D0872334

A THOROUGHLY EFFICIENT NAVY

WITHDRAWN
UTSA LIBRARIES

Studies in Defense Policy

STUDIES IN DEFENSE POLICY

A THOROUGHLY EFFICIENT NAVY

William W. Kaufmann

THE BROOKINGS INSTITUTION
Washington, D.C.

Copyright © 1987 by
THE BROOKINGS INSTITUTION
1775 Massachusetts Avenue, N.W., Washington, D.C. 20036

Library of Congress Cataloging-in-Publication data:

Kaufmann, William W.
  A thoroughly efficient Navy.
  (Studies in defense policy)
  1. United States. Navy. 2. United States—Military
policy. I. Title. II. Series.
VA58.4.K38 1987   359′.00973   87-11596
ISBN 0-8157-4845-0 (pbk.)

9 8 7 6 5 4 3 2 1

LIBRARY
The University of Texas
at San Antonio

Board of Trustees
Louis W. Cabot
Chairman
Ralph S. Saul
Vice Chairman;
Chairman, Executive Committee;
Chairman, Development Committee
Samuel H. Armacost
J. David Barnes
Rex J. Bates
Frank T. Cary
A. W. Clausen
William T. Coleman, Jr.
Lloyd N. Cutler
Thomas R. Donahue
Charles W. Duncan, Jr.
Walter Y. Elisha
Robert F. Erburu
Roberto C. Goizueta
Robert D. Haas
Philip M. Hawley
Roy M. Huffington
B. R. Inman
Vernon E. Jordan, Jr.
James A. Joseph
James T. Lynn
Donald F. McHenry
Bruce K. MacLaury
Mary Patterson McPherson
Maconda B. O'Connor
Donald S. Perkins
J. Woodward Redmond
James D. Robinson III
Robert V. Roosa
Henry B. Schacht
Howard R. Swearer
Morris Tanenbaum
James D. Wolfensohn
Ezra K. Zilkha
Charles J. Zwick

Honorary Trustees
Vincent M. Barnett, Jr.
Barton M. Biggs
Eugene R. Black
Robert D. Calkins
Edward W. Carter
Bruce B. Dayton
Douglas Dillon
Huntington Harris
Andrew Heiskell
Roger W. Heyns
John E. Lockwood
William McC. Martin, Jr.
Robert S. McNamara
Arjay Miller
Charles W. Robinson
H. Chapman Rose
Gerard C. Smith
Robert Brookings Smith
Sydney Stein, Jr.
Phyllis A. Wallace

THE BROOKINGS INSTITUTION is an independent organization devoted to nonpartisan research, education, and publication in economics, government, foreign policy, and the social sciences generally. Its principal purposes are to aid in the development of sound public policies and to promote public understanding of issues of national importance.

The Institution was founded on December 8, 1927, to merge the activities of the Institute for Government Research, founded in 1916, the Institute of Economics, founded in 1922, and the Robert Brookings Graduate School of Economics and Government, founded in 1924.

The Board of Trustees is responsible for the general administration of the Institution, while the immediate direction of the policies, program, and staff is vested in the President, assisted by an advisory committee of the officers and staff. The by-laws of the Institution state: "It is the function of the Trustees to make possible the conduct of scientific research, and publication, under the most favorable conditions, and to safeguard the independence of the research staff in the pursuit of their studies and in the publication of the results of such studies. It is not a part of their function to determine, control, or influence the conduct of particular investigations or the conclusions reached."

The President bears final responsibility for the decision to publish a manuscript as a Brookings book. In reaching his judgment on the competence, accuracy, and objectivity of each study, the President is advised by the director of the appropriate research program and weighs the views of a panel of expert outside readers who report to him in confidence on the quality of the work. Publication of a work signifies that it is deemed a competent treatment worthy of public consideration but does not imply endorsement of conclusions or recommendations.

The Institution maintains its position of neutrality on issues of public policy in order to safeguard the intellectual freedom of the staff. Hence interpretations or conclusions in Brookings publications should be understood to be solely those of the authors and should not be attributed to the Institution, to its trustees, officers, or other staff members, or to the organizations that support its research.

FOREWORD

As early as 1974 the United States Navy set the goal of a 600-ship fleet, at the heart of which would be 15 deployable aircraft carriers, 100 attack submarines, and the amphibious lift for 4 Marine Corps brigades and their supporting aircraft. President Reagan endorsed that goal in 1981. Since then, Congress has appropriated funds for more than 100 new ships, and the Navy hopes to reach its goal by 1989. However, recent reductions in the budgets of the Department of Defense, the prospect that defense appropriations will provide for little or no real growth during the next few years, and the need to retire a number of aging ships will make a 600-ship navy difficult to reach and sustain. These developments inevitably reopen the issue of whether the Navy has adequately justified the need for a 600-ship (or, more accurately, a 622-ship) fleet and what constitutes a balanced alternative to it, given the decisions already made by the Reagan administration and Congress.

In this study William W. Kaufmann describes the genesis of the 600-ship navy, questions the merits of the maritime strategy proposed by the Navy as the basis for the fleet, and examines the role of naval forces in nuclear deterrence, protection of the major sea-lanes, the projection of military power with carrier battle groups and amphibious forces, and peacetime patrols overseas. He concludes that a substantially less costly fleet of 570 ships, including 12 deployable aircraft carriers, 220 other surface combatants, the amphibious ships for 1 Marine amphibious force, and 96 nuclear-powered attack submarines, will fully meet the need for U.S. naval forces in the foreseeable future.

William W. Kaufmann is a consultant to the Brookings Foreign Policy Studies program and a member of the faculty of the John F. Kennedy School of Government at Harvard University. He is grateful to M. Staser Holcomb, Vice Admiral, USN (Ret.), Michael K. MccGwire, and John

D. Steinbruner for their comments on the manuscript. Caroline Lalire edited the manuscript, and Stephen K. Wegren verified its factual content. Kathryn Ho once again produced the manuscript with her unique combination of skill, intelligence, and patience. Funding for this study was provided in part by the Ford Foundation and by the John D. and Catherine T. MacArthur Foundation.

The views expressed in this study are those of the author and should not be ascribed to the persons or organizations whose assistance is acknowledged, or to the trustees, officers, or staff members of the Brookings Institution.

BRUCE K. MACLAURY
President

April 1987
Washington, D.C.

CONTENTS

Text Tables

A THOROUGHLY EFFICIENT NAVY

There is a homely adage which runs, "speak softly and carry a big stick; you will go far." If the American nation will speak softly and yet build and keep at a pitch of the highest training a thoroughly efficient navy, the Monroe Doctrine will go far.

THEODORE ROOSEVELT

CHAPTER ONE

DEFENSE AND THE NAVY

IT HAS been said that if all economists were laid end to end, they would not reach a conclusion, but that is probably unfair. Most, if not all, of them would agree that defense is the classic public good. Unlike a meal, national defense cannot be bought and enjoyed by one person to the exclusion of all others. In principle, defense protects the entire nation. All citizens allegedly benefit from it; none has an incentive to pay for it. Consequently, as the Constitution of the United States dictates, the federal government provides the common defense, and taxes and borrows to pay for it. In performing these functions, as the saying goes, public officials engage in choice without the benefit of markets.

Supply and Demand

Despite the theory, buyers and sellers do emerge as the government goes about acquiring the armed forces of the United States. The private sector (though handsomely compensated in various ways) provides most of the goods and many of the services sought by the Department of Defense. Arsenals owned and operated by the government are largely a thing of the past. Major corporations such as General Dynamics, McDonnell Douglas, and Boeing compete to build the missiles, aircraft, tanks, and ships that are the sinews of defense. Within the Department of Defense itself, the secretary of defense is the president of a vast conglomerate, with hundreds of billions of dollars at his disposal, while the three great and supposedly subsidiary military departments—the Army, the Navy, and the Air Force—eagerly compete to relieve him of those resources. And then, of course, there is the Congress of the United States, which ultimately decides how much money will go to the

1

departments and how they will use it. Even so, it is the exception rather than the rule that Congress changes annual defense budget authority by more than a few percentage points or significantly alters the allocations proposed by the secretary of defense. Whether the coming years will afford one of those exceptions still remains to be seen.

Although markets may not exist in any formal sense, buyers have ways to determine how products compare in price and performance. Warfare is the most decisive arbiter of those issues. Most societies lack a strong taste for the institution, however, and nuclear weapons have understandably diminished it. As a substitute, planners both inside and outside the Department of Defense have devised simulations of war—in the field and on paper. Units conduct maneuvers and exercises; weapons undergo a variety of tests and comparisons; calculations attempt to show what constitute the preferred size and composition of a force, whether for combat or for deterrence. Since no one has yet obtained any military experience and judgment from having fought a nuclear war, and since most senior officers do not practice their profession with great frequency in the more traditional forms of combat, these substitutes inevitably exercise an influence. In effect, they serve as the "consumer reports" that help shape the demand for military goods and services.

Despite the availability of these reports, it is the subsidiaries rather than the secretary of defense and his staff that dominate this peculiar marketplace. Not only do they specify in detail the products they want and advertise their merits; they also manage to infiltrate the ranks of the executive suite. Rare is the staff in the Office of the Secretary of Defense that does not have representatives of the three military departments as members. Rarer still is the case in which the secretary of defense's decisions on what to buy are not influenced to an important degree by these representatives. In the circumstances, it is hardly surprising that, lacking a strong secretary of defense, the military departments fail to create a coordinated and rational set of demands or that current efforts to reform defense decisionmaking will make these subsidiaries even more difficult to control in the future.

The Department of the Navy as Subsidiary

Among the most fascinating and controversial of the purchasers is the Department of the Navy. Much of the fascination comes from its being

Table 1-1. **Defense Budget Authority by Major Component, Fiscal Years 1978–86**

Component	1978	1979	1980	1981	1982	1983	1984	1985	1986
	Billions of fiscal 1987 dollars								
Army	48.2	49.2	49.4	55.7	62.2	66.0	76.3	79.4	74.9
Navy[a]	67.0	65.5	65.7	73.0	83.7	93.1	96.6	105.6	98.0
Air Force	56.0	55.1	57.9	66.2	73.7	83.7	100.2	105.9	97.5
Defense agencies/OSD[b]	6.8	6.9	7.7	9.5	11.0	10.6	11.9	14.0	15.6
Defense-wide[c]	18.5	19.3	19.7	21.3	21.8	19.4	0.6[c]	1.0	1.9
Total	196.5	196.0	200.4	225.7	252.4	272.8	285.6	306.0	288.0
	Percent								
Army	24.5	25.1	24.7	24.7	24.6	24.2	26.7	26.0	26.0
Navy[a]	34.1	33.4	32.8	32.3	33.1	34.1	33.8	34.5	34.0
Air Force	28.5	28.1	28.9	29.3	29.2	30.7	35.1	34.6	33.9
Defense agencies/OSD[b]	3.5	3.5	3.8	4.2	4.4	3.9	4.2	4.6	5.4
Defense-wide[c]	9.4	9.8	9.8	9.4	8.6	7.1	0.2	0.3	0.7

Source: Office of the Assistant Secretary of Defense (Comptroller), *National Defense Budget Estimates for FY 1987*, p. 100.

a. Includes budget authority for the U.S. Marine Corps.
b. Office of the Secretary of Defense.
c. The sharp decline in defense-wide budget authority results from allocating military retired pay to the other components.

a not-so-small replica of the Department of Defense. It has its own army in the form of the U.S. Marine Corps. It has its own navy, naturally. And it actually has three air forces: one for the Marine Corps, one that sails about on the Navy's aircraft carriers, and one that is land based and engages primarily in antisubmarine warfare (ASW). It even has its own nuclear forces made up of fleet ballistic missile submarines and a substantial array of shorter-range nuclear delivery systems that can be launched from carriers, surface combatants, and attack submarines. As might be expected, it also owns or rents a number of ships that it uses to transport cargo, deploy reinforcements overseas, and pre-position weapons, equipment, and supplies near some of the more troubled regions of the world. Since neither the Army nor the Air Force has managed to accumulate such a diversified portfolio of capabilities, it is little wonder that the Navy consistently earns more than a third of the defense budget (see table 1-1).

Such diversity and such a large market share inevitably make the Navy controversial as well. Like most corporations, the three main military services prefer monopoly positions as they compete for the defense dollar. Thus the Army claims the role of ground combat, and the Air Force tries to establish exclusive rights to operations in air and space. The Navy, because it is such a conglomerate, not only commands a monopoly over everything that moves on or under the seas, but also penetrates the markets of the other two services by insisting that anything launched from a ship—whether ground forces, aircraft, or missiles—must belong to the Navy. It has even managed to establish a claim to land-based forces with its patrol aircraft, on the ground that their main mission is to destroy submarines at sea. The upshot is overlap and friction as the Army periodically questions the utility of the Marine Corps, and the Air Force denigrates the efficiency of carrier-based aircraft.

Technology has sharpened these controversies. The advent of long-range bombers and aerial refueling means that, even without overseas bases, the Air Force can attack targets that previously only carrier-based aircraft could reach. Airlift aircraft permit the Army to move units to distant areas more swiftly than the Navy can move ship-based Marines. What is more, with improvements in surveillance and ordnance, ships are becoming easier to disable or destroy from high-flying aircraft firing from a distance of several hundred miles. One consequence is that the Navy now devotes an increasing share of its resources to the defense of its offensive capabilities. Another is that the Navy must justify these capabilities either by an appeal to tradition and emotion or on the ground that it can perform functions the Army and Air Force are unable either to duplicate or to conduct at lower cost. The task is not easy to accomplish when a carrier battle group with the offensive firepower of one Air Force fighter-attack wing or less costs at least 50 percent more and is easier under most conditions to put out of action.

Controversy even surrounds that most traditional of naval functions: protection of the sea-lanes over which the men, equipment, and supplies must move to sustain a distant conventional war. For many years, with enlightened self-interest, the high command of the Navy resisted the doctrine of the Eisenhower administration that major conflicts of the future would be fought with nuclear weapons. Having sensibly helped to overturn that doctrine, the naval establishment soon encountered the view that a conventional war between the superpowers, like the Arab-Israeli campaigns, would last for no more than a few days or weeks. After that, so the assertion went, the exhausted belligerents would either collapse or resort in desperation to the tactical and then the strategic use of nuclear weapons. Whichever the outcome, the forces overseas would hardly need much in the way of resupply, and airlift would be able to provide these modest amounts. The traditional Navy, on which the nation is spending so many billions, would find little or nothing to do in such circumstances.

The Future of the Navy

Conceivably this view of future warfare is correct. Conceivably surface navies—at least as they are known—are about to become obsolete. But hard evidence on that score is still lacking. The United States committed a force of eight divisions to the war in Korea and fought for several years without any recourse to nuclear arms. A U.S. force of roughly the same size ended up in Vietnam and also engaged in nonnuclear combat for many years. In both conflicts the demand for reinforcements, replacements, and resupply proved extensive. In both engagements 95 percent of the tonnage needed to support ground and air operations went by sea. On neither occasion, admittedly, did the opponent possess nuclear weapons, although the Soviet Union, at least in the second instance, could have readily supplied them. Nor did a potential enemy threaten the sea lines of communication (SLOCs) to Korea or Vietnam. But the United States had to allow for the possibility that the threat to the SLOCs would materialize and that U.S. naval forces would be needed to protect its shipping.

The future could evolve differently. The fact remains, nonetheless, that the Soviet Union continues to maintain, modernize, and in some respects expand its navy. It is also true that no power has used nuclear weapons in combat since 1945. At some later date it may turn out that navies in their traditional form no longer have a major role to play in defense and deterrence. In the meantime it would be risky indeed to forgo a large part of naval capabilities. For the foreseeable future policymakers and force planners will have to decide, not *whether* the United States should maintain a traditional navy, but what its size and composition should be.

The issue is not a new one. The Marine Corps, it is true, enjoys the good fortune of a law passed in 1952 which dictates that the corps, at a minimum, shall consist of three divisions and their associated air wings.[1] However, the rest of the Navy lacks any such legal protection. Furthermore, it cannot simply live with its inherited capabilities. As a general rule its ships and submarines have service lives of about thirty years, and its aircraft need to be replaced, on the average, every twenty years.

1. Martin Binkin and Jeffrey Record, *Where Does the Marine Corps Go from Here?* (Brookings, 1976), pp. 7–8.

Table 1-2. U.S. Naval Ships Decommissioned and Net Reduction in the Fleet, 1968–75

Category	Number decomissioned	New ships[a]	Net reduction
Antisubmarine warfare carrier	8	. . .	8
Amphibious ships	123	23	100
Attack submarines	59	29	30
Destroyers and frigates	181	46	135
Underway replenishment ships	n.a.	n.a.	32
Mine countermeasures ships	81	. . .	81[b]
Total	n.a.	n.a.	386

Source: *Department of Defense Annual Report, Fiscal Year 1977*, pp. 156–57.
n.a. Not available.
a. All new ships were larger and more powerful than their predecessors.
b. Most of these ships were decommissioned, but a few were transferred to the naval reserve fleet.

Consequently, the Navy, like its sister services, must design a program and struggle annually for a budget that not only establishes a force of a certain size and composition but also maintains and modernizes it as threats change and the older equipment must be replaced.

The future size and composition of the fleet became a major issue toward the end of the 1960s. By that time, according to the Senate Armed Services Committee, the Navy deployed a total of 976 active commissioned ships, up from 917 in fiscal 1964, before the United States became an active participant in the Vietnam War.[2] But despite a substantial shipbuilding program, especially during the 1960s, a large part of the Navy—built during World War II—was nearing the end of its useful service life and in need of replacement if the fleet was to approximate its prewar size. Indeed, at least 484 ships were to be decommissioned or transferred to the naval reserve between 1968 and 1975 (see table 1-2). To complicate matters further, the new ships on the drawing boards or already funded were larger, more capable, and much more costly in real terms than their predecessors. Consequently, Navy planners had to recognize that replacements could not be made on a one-for-one basis and that the size of the fleet would have to shrink. The issue, accordingly, was where the shrinkage should stop and what the composition of the smaller navy would be. In 1969 Admiral Thomas H. Moorer, then chief of naval operations (the equivalent of chief of staff of the Army or Air Force) thought the size of the fleet should stabilize at 850 ships. His

2. *Fiscal Year 1972, Authorization for Military Procurement, Research and Development, Construction and Real Estate Acquisition for the Safeguard ABM and Reserve Strengths*, Hearings before the Senate Armed Services Committee, 99 Cong. 1 sess. (Government Printing Office, 1971), pt. 1, p. 908.

Table 1-3. Planned U.S. 600-Ship Navy, Fiscal Year 1975

Type	Number
Ballistic missile submarines	41
Strategic support ships	6
Aircraft carriers	12
Sea control ships[a]	8
Major surface combatants	250
Nuclear-powered attack submarines	90
Amphibious ships	66
Mine countermeasures ships	9
Underway replenishment ships	56
Auxiliaries	62
Total	600

Source: *Department of Defense Annual Report, Fiscal Year 1975*, pp. 57–60, 118, 122, 126, 136, 139, 140–42.
a. A sea control ship was intended to be a small carrier (about 20,000 tons displacement) capable of launching a small number of vertical-takeoff-and-landing aircraft and helicopters. None was ever built.

successor, Admiral Elmo R. Zumwalt, Jr., set the floor at 770. By 1975 James R. Schlesinger, then secretary of defense, accepted Admiral James L. Holloway III's recommendation of what was to become the most cherished goal of the Navy: 600 ships.[3] An estimate of its composition is shown in table 1-3.

Although a fleet of 600 ships represents a brilliantly rounded number, it understates the actual goal of the Navy. In fact, in a study known as "Sea Plan 2000," completed in the late 1970s, naval authorities stated a somewhat more ambitious objective of 631 ships. Of that total, 585 would be in the active fleet and the remaining 46 in the naval reserve. At the heart of this force were to be 15 aircraft carriers (of which 1 at all times would be in the so-called service life extension program, or SLEP) with their 112 escorts, and 55 underway replenishment ships with their 40 escorts, for a total of 222 ships. In addition, the plan proposed the amphibious lift for one-and-a-half Marine amphibious forces ($1\frac{1}{2}$ divisions and their air squadrons), consisting of 78 ships and 18 escorts, as well as 98 nuclear-powered attack submarines (SSNs), 25 fleet ballistic missile submarines (SSBNs), and 61 support ships of various kinds.[4] For all practical purposes, this fleet was the forebear of the so-called 600-ship navy that is now taking shape.

3. Barry M. Blechman, Edward M. Gramlich, and Robert W. Hartman, *Setting National Priorities: The 1976 Budget* (Brookings, 1975), p. 108; and *Department of Defense Annual Report, Fiscal Year 1975*, pp. 117–42.
4. Office of the Secretary of the Navy, "Sea Plan 2000 (U)," Naval Force Planning Study, Washington, D.C., March 1978.

The actual birth of the 600-ship navy followed its conception by more than five years. The Ford administration attempted to father it in 1976, but Congress was not in the mood. The Carter administration refused to consider it in general and rejected "Sea Plan 2000" in particular. Meanwhile the size of the Navy continued to decline as more ships were retired than new ones were commissioned. The actual size of the decrease depends on which ships are included in the fleet. According to the counting rules introduced by the new secretary of the Navy, John F. Lehman, Jr., in 1981, the so-called deployable battle forces (a mixture of active and reserve ships) had declined to a low of 479 ships by fiscal 1980. If other reserve ships and auxiliaries are included in the count, as was the custom until 1981, the total fleet consisted of 531 ships.[5]

Whatever the right number, it represented the end of a decade of shrinkage in the size of the Navy, regardless of what the incoming Reagan administration might decide to do. Many fewer ships would have to be retired during most of the 1980s than had been decommissioned during the 1970s. Furthermore, both the Ford and the Carter administrations had provided the funding for a substantial number of new ships, more than would have to be decommissioned. Consequently, the fleet was bound to start growing again, though it was not scheduled to reach the 600-ship goal as defined by Secretary Lehman.

The Reagan Program

With the advent of the Reagan administration, the shipbuilding program underwent a dramatic change. In his last report to Congress, in January 1981, Secretary of Defense Harold Brown proposed to fund 80 new ships between fiscal 1982 and 1986, including 14 in fiscal 1982. With President Reagan giving a strong endorsement to the 600-ship navy, Secretary of Defense Caspar W. Weinberger increased new ship construction from 14 to 17 in fiscal 1982 and recommended funding another 133 between fiscal 1983 and 1987. Thus while Brown sought to build an average of 16 new ships a year, Weinberger set his sights on an average of 25 ships a year.[6]

The original plan underwent a number of reductions in successive

---

5. *Department of Defense Annual Report, Fiscal Year 1987*, pp. 179, 324.

6. *Department of Defense Annual Report, Fiscal Year 1982*, p. 171, and *Fiscal Year 1983*, p. III-36.

Table 1-4. The U.S. Navy's Force Structure Goals for Deployable Battle Force Ships in Fiscal Year 1987

Type	Number
Ballistic missile submarines	20–40[a]
Deployable aircraft carriers	15
Reactivated battleships	4
Principal surface combatants	238
Nuclear-powered attack submarines	100
Mine countermeasures ships	14
Amphibious ships	75
Patrol combatants	6
Underway replenishment ships	65
Support ships and other auxiliaries	60–65[a]
Total	597–622

Source: *Department of Defense Annual Report, Fiscal Year 1987*, p. 179.
a. The eventual goal for ballistic missile submarines had not been determined. The eventual number will presumably depend on such factors as the strategic arms reductions talks and the service lives of the older ballistic missile submarines. The number of support ships and auxiliaries will also depend, presumably, on the number of ballistic missile submarines in commission.

years. Whereas Weinberger had first called for the funding of 38 new ships in fiscal 1987, in his actual request for fiscal 1987 (submitted in early February 1986) he proposed funding only 21 new ships. All told, between fiscal 1982 and fiscal 1986, Congress funded 105 major new ships rather than the 150 originally requested. Even so, budget authority for the Department of the Navy increased in real terms by 49 percent between fiscal 1980 and 1986 (for a cumulative six-year total of $550 billion, in constant dollars), and the secretary of the navy continued to insist that enough ships had already been funded to ensure the deployment of 600 battle force ships by 1990.[7]

The secretary of defense did not contradict him. But he did note in his report to Congress for fiscal 1987 that, although "inflationary pressures continue to inhibit progress toward the Navy's 600-ship goal, the Five Year Program still permits some growth in the level of naval forces." Elsewhere in the same report he specified the Navy's goals (as shown in table 1-4) and observed, "By the end of the decade, many parts of this force structure will be in place. The Navy will have built a force of 15 deployable aircraft carriers, returned to service four modernized battleships, and expanded the attack submarine force to 100 ships. Other goals will not be achieved until the 1990s, however. For example, the

7. *Department of Defense Annual Report, Fiscal Year 1987*, pp. 178, 194; and Office of the Assistant Secretary of Defense (Comptroller), *National Defense Budget Estimates for FY 1987*, p. 100.

amphibious lift objective will not be met until 1996, a two-year delay necessitated by funding reductions. Likewise, requirements for mine warfare and support ships will not be fulfilled until the early to mid-1990s, when the last of the ships in the FY 1987–91 program are delivered . . . the Navy will also fall short of its goal of 238 principal surface combatants.'' Furthermore, the reserve component of the deployable battle forces, according to this plan, would grow from 6 ships in fiscal 1982 to 51 ships by fiscal 1992, presumably because of shortages in personnel and operating funds.[8]

The Issues

These comments and data indicate why, despite the assurances of the secretary of the navy, the size and composition of the Navy remain unsettled. And there are good reasons why the issue will not disappear in the immediate future. During the 1990s a large number of cruisers and destroyers will reach the end of their useful service lives. The Navy will also need a great many new aircraft and helicopters to go with a greatly expanded fleet. Indeed, Secretary Lehman has estimated that his department will have to obtain annual real increases in its budget of 3 percent for some years to come to sustain the fleet at 600 or more ships and meet these other demands. The Congressional Budget Office, for its part, calculated in 1985 that the required real increase could run as high as 6 percent a year for at least ten years.[9] At the same time, the constraints imposed on the defense budget by the federal deficit—the Gramm-Rudman-Hollings Balanced Budget and Emergency Deficit Control Act of 1985—and President Reagan's reluctance to raise taxes make it unlikely that defense resources during the coming four or more years will grow enough even to cover the effects of inflation. The upshot is that the Navy will either have to live with much less than the 3 percent real growth deemed necessary by its secretary or obtain the growth at the expense of the other services—an unlikely prospect.

Because of these circumstances it is not simply an academic exercise

8. *Department of Defense Annual Report, Fiscal Year 1987*, pp. 179–80.

9. Admiral James D. Watkins, U.S. Navy, *The Maritime Strategy* (Annapolis: U.S. Naval Institute, 1986), pp. 35–36; and Peter T. Tarpgaard and Robert E. Mechanic, *Future Budget Requirements for the 600-Ship Navy* (Congressional Budget Office, 1985), pp. 66–68.

to ask about the importance of the 600-ship navy to the interests and security of the United States. The secretary of the navy himself has seen fit to raise the issue even more explicitly and asks a number of specific questions. "Do we really need so many ships? Are the Navy and Marine Corps effective in helping to deter Soviet aggression—across the full spectrum of violence, from terrorism to nuclear war? Do we have a strategy that guides the planning and training of our forces? Is it the correct strategy? If it is, are we building the right types and numbers of ships to execute it? Finally, can this nation afford to sustain a 600-ship fleet—not only well-equipped but properly manned—for the long term?"[10]

They are good questions. They deserve answers.

10. Watkins, *Maritime Strategy,* p. 32.

CHAPTER TWO

THE MARITIME STRATEGY

FOR MORE than a decade, the Navy itself has sought in one way or another to answer the questions raised by its current secretary. During most of the 1970s and all of the early 1980s, spokesmen for the Navy emphasized the extent of international turbulence and the worldwide responsibilities of the United States. They reported on the growing size and activity of the Russian navy. They stressed the importance of maintaining U.S. naval deployments in the Mediterranean, the Atlantic, the western Pacific, and, more recently, the Indian Ocean and the Arabian Sea in the vicinity of the Persian Gulf. From this background of a troubled international scene, an expanding Soviet threat, and the need to maintain a worldwide naval presence, they asserted the "requirement" of a 600-ship navy with its 15 large-deck aircraft carriers, 100 attack submarines, 78 amphibious ships, and the several hundred cruisers and destroyers needed to escort the main fighting forces.

Congress proved willing to support the commitment of the Reagan administration to the 600-ship navy. But nagging questions kept occurring about how navy force planners made the leap from observations about turbulent times, worldwide interests, and an aggressive Soviet Union to the particular size and composition of the fleet the Navy had so persistently sought. And the questions grew sharper as the costs of large ships began to make long-range bombers, missiles, and wide-bodied cargo aircraft look like bargains. The price of a Trident submarine with its 24 ballistic missiles was running to well over $2 billion; a Nimitz-class nuclear-powered aircraft carrier without its aircraft had risen to more than $3.5 billion before it ever left port; and even modern cruisers and destroyers (without nuclear power but with advanced radars and battle management systems) had passed the billion-dollar mark, while the latest nuclear-powered attack submarines (of the Los Angeles class) with all their gear were approaching that level. What were those forces doing that other and cheaper ones could not do equally well?

The Navy could demonstrate, as a response, that in most crises since World War II (minor as well as major) American presidents had regarded it as the service of choice to deal with the situation. It could also show, perhaps less conclusively, that of all the weapons systems at their disposal, presidents liked aircraft carriers the best. Unfortunately, however, the Navy did not succeed in demonstrating that the presence of U.S. naval forces made much difference to the resolution of those crises. In particular, the role of aircraft carriers as premier peacekeepers remained in dispute. This uncertainty inevitably raises the question: if peacetime patrol and crisis management are the main functions of the U.S. Navy, why are so many expensive fighting ships necessary to the effectiveness of the fleet?

David Lloyd George once said, "A fully equipped Duke costs as much to keep up as two Dreadnoughts, and Dukes are just as great a terror, and they last longer." The United States has no dukes of its own to dispose of, but it can deploy a variety of vessels that are cheaper than aircraft carriers and that can perform equally well if their main purpose is to maintain a peacetime presence and symbolize American power.

War and Peace

The difficulty of resting a force as large and expensive as the 600-ship fleet on a foundation as small and fragile as peacetime presence had persuaded the Navy well before 1986 to try a different tack. Not only did it need to establish its proposed force on the more solid basis of its wartime missions; it also had to relate the size and composition of the fleet to the performance of those missions. The most significant product of this recognition was the publication of *The Maritime Strategy* in January 1986.[1]

The Maritime Strategy is a remarkable document. It deserves the most careful consideration, not only because its arguments are impor-

---

1. Admiral James D. Watkins, U.S. Navy, *The Maritime Strategy* (Annapolis: U.S. Naval Institute, 1986). The three main chapters of the book are "The Maritime Strategy," by Watkins, pp. 2–17; "The Amphibious Warfare Strategy," by General P. X. Kelley, USMC, and Major Hugh K. O'Donnell, Jr., USMC, pp. 18–29; and "The 600-Ship Navy," by John F. Lehman, Jr., pp. 30–40.

tant, but also because its three principal signatories were the chief of naval operations, the commandant of the United States Marine Corps, and the secretary of the navy.

Admiral James D. Watkins, chief of naval operations at the time, takes the lead in describing and defending the maritime strategy. He makes the usual bow to the need for international peace and stability, and to the Navy's contribution to them through its worldwide presence. But he insists that the heart of the maritime strategy lies in what he calls crisis response; that is, the ability of the Navy to help contain and control a crisis before it escalates into open warfare. However, what he concentrates on for the most part is what he describes as the three phases of the strategy: deterrence, or the transition to war; seizing the initiative; and carrying the fight to the enemy. Phases two and three deserve the closest scrutiny, since they supposedly provide the main foundations for the 600-ship navy. But certain aspects of the first phase, in which U.S. naval and Marine forces engage in rapid forward deployment, warrant careful study as well.

The war visualized by Admiral Watkins, presumably for force planning purposes, has the Soviet Union and, one supposes, its allies in the Warsaw Pact attacking NATO forces in an effort to obtain a rapid conquest of Europe. He concedes that other Soviet surrogates and clients may also engage in simultaneous attacks, but he believes that Soviet military planners would prefer to concentrate on one theater of war at a time. Although this reasoning seems to imply that the Army and the Air Force should prepare for only one major contingency in their force planning, he regards the Navy's role as worldwide and demanding.

In these circumstances U.S. naval and Marine amphibious forces would have four missions: to deny "the Soviets their kind of war by exerting global pressure"; to destroy the Soviet navy; to "influence the land battle" in Europe by tying down Soviet forces in other parts of the Soviet Union, by ensuring the reinforcement and resupply of NATO's land and tactical air forces, and by the direct use of carrier and Marine amphibious power in the land campaign against the Warsaw Pact; and finally, to "terminate the war" on terms acceptable to the United States and its allies through such measures as threatening to attack the Soviet homeland or to reduce Soviet strategic nuclear forces by sinking Soviet fleet ballistic missile submarines.[2]

2. Ibid., p. 14.

To achieve these four objectives, Admiral Watkins assumes that U.S. naval forces will destroy their Soviet counterparts in the Mediterranean, Indian Ocean, and other forward areas, "neutralize" Soviet clients (if required), and fight their way "toward Soviet home waters." Furthermore, as carrier battle groups and other units move forward, "we will wage an aggressive campaign against all Soviet submarines, including ballistic missile submarines." Admiral Watkins hastens to add, however, that the strategy "does not envision automatic attacks on any specific targets," even though the United States "cannot allow our adversary to assume he will be able to attack the fleet with impunity, from inviolable sanctuaries."[3]

General Paul X. Kelley, the commandant of the Marine Corps and second signatory of *The Maritime Strategy,* stresses many of the same themes as Admiral Watkins, but adds some interesting initiatives of his own. He talks of bringing the Soviet Union "to the negotiating table as quickly as possible, on terms that are favorable to the West," and visualizes naval operations "on the exposed Rimland flanks" and striking rapidly "at key Soviet pressure points in a campaign of nautical maneuver." Furthermore, because a "stout NATO defense" contains the Warsaw Pact in the central region of Europe, massed amphibious task forces, together with supporting battleship surface action groups, will be able to "undertake landings to retake conquered territory and to seize key objectives in the Soviet rear. Operating as a component of the naval campaign, MAGTFs [Marine air-ground task forces] could land on the North Cape, the eastern Baltic or the Black Sea coasts, in the Kuriles, or on Sakhalin Island—thereby adding a crucial measure of leverage to the successful conduct of the maritime campaign." General Kelley even goes so far as to suggest that naval forces used in this manner "can make the strategic difference."[4]

Some Issues

The Duke of Wellington once said, upon receiving a draft of soldiers shipped to him in Spain, "I don't know what effect these men will have upon the enemy, but, by God, they terrify me." Critics no doubt will

3. Ibid., pp. 11, 12.
4. Ibid., p. 26.

react in much the same way to *The Maritime Strategy*. To what extent the strategy justifies such a reaction is debatable. Admiral Watkins asserts that it is "a forward strategy, [in] keeping with the national policy of forward defense and drawing on the forward-deployed posture and rapid mobility of naval forces." He also insists that it is "fully consistent with the national strategy documents and directives of this [the Reagan] administration which emphasize the importance of maritime superiority to our national defense."[5]

Conceivably Admiral Watkins is correct, but no one can be quite sure on that score. In 1982 Secretary of Defense Weinberger enunciated a wartime strategy "that confronts the enemy, were he to attack, with the risk of our counteroffensive against his vulnerable points." By 1984, however, the secretary was in a mood to limit the scope, duration, and intensity of a conflict and to declare that, should deterrence fail, "general strategic priorities, specific circumstances, and forces available at the time would govern force employment." A year later he indicated that "our preference would be to end hostilities by employing forces that do not create or risk escalation." By 1986, almost coincident with publication of *The Maritime Strategy,* he went on to say, "The most important truth about the recent buildup is that we have been buying and fielding forces to implement policies and strategies over which there was little disagreement between this Administration and its predecessor."[6] It remains less than clear, in short, that the maritime strategy, for which the Carter administration had no sympathy (at least in its earlier incarnation) has the sanction claimed for it by Admiral Watkins.

This lack of formal blessing should hardly come as a surprise to the Navy. Senior officers should know from experience that in an era shadowed by the threat of nuclear exchanges, even secretaries of defense are more likely to want to test gingerly the cold waters of contemporary warfare than to plunge intrepidly into their depths. Yet *The Maritime Strategy* calls for precisely that kind of a plunge. In fact, according to Admiral Watkins, implementation of the strategy requires "appropriate rules of engagement at the brink of war to avoid losing the battle of the first salvo which is so important in Soviet doctrine."[7] In somewhat plainer language, that seems to mean that naval commanders must have

5. Ibid., p. 15.

6. *Department of Defense Annual Report, Fiscal Year 1983,* p. I-16, *Fiscal Year 1985,* p. 38, *Fiscal Year 1986,* p. 27, and *Fiscal Year 1987,* p. 37.

7. Watkins, *Maritime Strategy,* p. 12.

the authority to fire first if war seems imminent. This hardly seems a contribution to the international stability and crisis control so highly prized by Admiral Watkins.

Predelegation is not the only way the strategy forces the president's hand. According to Admiral Watkins, "Keys to the success of both the initial phase and the strategy as a whole are speed and decisiveness in national decisionmaking." Prompt decisions "are needed to permit rapid forward deployment of additional forces in crisis." And execution of the president's authority to call up reservists (currently limited to 100,000 in number) becomes increasingly crucial to successful implementation of the strategy.[8]

As if this were not inducement enough for a president to question the proposed strategy in a crisis, Admiral Watkins offers an even stronger one. As he sees it, "The Soviets [whoever specifically they may be] place great weight on the nuclear correlation of forces, even during the time before nuclear weapons have been used." Consequently, maritime forces engaged in a forward strategy "can influence that correlation, both by destroying Soviet ballistic missile submarines and by improving our own nuclear posture, through deployment of carriers and Tomahawk [cruise missile] platforms around the periphery of the Soviet Union."[9] To Admiral Watkins, such measures would not lead immediately to nuclear war, and he could be right. The evidence about the causes of an escalation to nuclear exchanges is sparse, to say the least. But it seems doubtful, in light of the uncertainty over just what would happen in those tense circumstances, that a president would commit himself in advance to any such steps or want force planning to proceed on any such assumptions.

Some Anomalies

The Maritime Strategy contains several anomalies as well as a number of exacting "requirements." General Kelley, for example, claims, "Making a case for an offensively oriented Navy and Marine Corps is not an easy undertaking if Europe is the primary U.S. area of interest." Yet the maritime strategy, as Admiral Watkins points out, is a response

8. Ibid., pp. 9–10.
9. Ibid., p. 14.

precisely to "a combined-arms assault against Europe." Again, General Kelley speaks of an enemy exhausted and contained "by a stout NATO defense" in the central region of Europe. Secretary of the Navy Lehman, on the other hand, claims that to discard maritime superiority (which he omits to define) "in an attempt to match the larger Soviet ground forces . . . would give us neither conventional deterrence on land nor secure access by sea unless the Western democracies are prepared to militarize their societies to an unprecedented, and unwise, degree."[10]

General Kelley also foresees massed naval task forces attacking "Soviet forces and their supporting infrastructure in Eastern Europe," even though sixteen years ago Secretary of the Navy John H. Chafee confessed that whereas aircraft carriers have their role in the European area, "in Europe, land-based air clearly has the advantage." Admiral Watkins, for his part, does not argue that the strategy implies "some immediate 'Charge of the Light Brigade' attack on the Kola peninsula or any other specific target," although he later insists that the Navy "must defeat Soviet maritime strength in all its dimensions, including base support."[11]

What is to be made of *The Maritime Strategy* in light of all these claims and counterclaims? The strategy it proposes seems to smack more of nostalgia than of reality. Perhaps unwittingly, its authors appear to have borrowed from the naval campaigns in the Pacific during World War II and Winston Churchill's pleas for attacks on the "soft underbelly" of Europe without ever asking whether the Soviet Union would lend itself to the same treatment as Japan and Germany, or questioning whether resources are likely to be at all commensurate with these objectives. Indeed, it is almost as though they "had been eight years upon a project for extracting sunbeams out of cucumbers, which were to be put into phials hermetically sealed, and let out to warm the air in raw inclement summers."[12]

Admiral Watkins no doubt would respond that "the Maritime Strategy recognizes that the unified and specified commanders fight the wars, under the direction of the President and the Secretary of Defense, and thus does not purport to be a detailed war plan with firm timelines, tactical doctrine, or specific target sets. Instead, it offers a global

---

10. Ibid., pp. 23, 7, 26, 37.
11. Ibid., pp. 26, 10, 11; and John H. Chafee, "Address of May 22, 1970," p. 3.
12. Jonathan Swift, *Gulliver's Travels,* chap. 5.

perspective to operational commanders and provides a foundation for advice to the National Command Authorities."[13]

Force Planning

Despite this caveat, Admiral Watkins notes that the maritime strategy "has become a key element in shaping Navy programmatic decisions." Secretary Lehman goes a step further in saying that "strategy's role is to give coherence and direction to the process of allocating money among competing types of ships and aircraft and different accounts for spare parts, missile systems, defense planning, and the training of forces. It provides guidelines to aid us in allocating both resources and shortages."[14]

Whether the maritime strategy, in fact, can do anything of the sort is dubious. Out of the 554 ships currently counted as deployable battle forces, 44 (or 8 percent) represent the Navy's contribution to the U.S. strategic nuclear deterrent. Yet *The Maritime Strategy* does not discuss them at all. If one is to believe what the secretary says about the rest of the Navy, the other ships in the 600-ship fleet rest on an intellectual foundation that is, at best, shaky.

The secretary describes the responsibilities of the four main U.S. fleets—the Sixth, the Second, the Seventh, and the Third—in some detail, at least as they are seen by the Navy. He does not, however, indicate the planning contingencies in the Mediterranean, the Atlantic, the western Pacific, the Indian Ocean, or the Bering Sea. He does not specify the size and composition of the threats that the Navy might encounter in those contingencies. Nor does he describe what role allied naval forces might have in the planning. If there are linkages among contingencies, enemy forces, allied contributions, missions, and U.S. naval capabilities, the secretary does not reveal them. Instead, alas, like so many of his predecessors, he engages in force planning by assertion.

Secretary Lehman's analysis of the Sixth Fleet's "requirements" is a good example of how this process works. First, he explains that the Sixth Fleet operates in the Mediterranean, where it can execute a number of missions on the southern flank of NATO and also support U.S. friends

---

13. Watkins, *Maritime Strategy*, p. 4.
14. Ibid., pp. 4, 36.

and allies in the Middle East. Then he states that, in wartime, "U.S. forces in the Sixth Fleet would have to include three or four carrier battle groups, operating to meet NATO commitments. We would also need to deploy a battleship surface action group and two underway replenishment groups."[15] Why it should be three or four carrier battle groups rather than five, or two, or none, the secretary fails to explain.

He treats the other three fleets in the same fashion. The United States must plan to have four or five carrier battle groups in the Second Fleet, another four in the Seventh Fleet, and two more in the Third Fleet, which is responsible for operations in the Bering Sea, the Eastern Pacific, and the mid-Pacific region as well as off Alaska and the Aleutian Islands, presumably in cooperation with the U.S. Air Force.

All in all, on the basis of this kind of analysis, the Navy must deploy the forces shown in table 2-1. In addition, according to the secretary, the Navy has a "requirement" for 100 attack submarines, "an adequate number of ballistic missile submarines," and the amphibious lift for the assault echelons of a Marine amphibious force (a division and its air wing) plus a Marine amphibious brigade.[16] He does not explain, however, what they would be expected to do. General Kelley, by contrast, does describe how he would use the amphibious forces. With the assault echelons of four Marine brigades, he would defend northern Norway and attack the perimeter of the Soviet Union at several different points, thereby preventing the reinforcement of Soviet units in Europe and hastening the collapse of the Soviet empire. Since the Soviet Union might have as many as 100 of its relatively small divisions deployed around its periphery (besides the forces committed to invading Europe), General Kelley's mission seems to be grossly disproportionate to the resources provided for the maritime strategy, even though the resources consist of the Marines.

Perhaps a closer connection exists between the rest of the forces and the objectives described by *The Maritime Strategy* than its authors reveal. But considering that the strategy, such as it is, emerged a decade after the first debut of the 600-ship navy, it is bound to raise questions about cause and effect. Clearly the gleam of the 600-ship navy existed long before the birth of the maritime strategy, although that does not make the size and composition of the fleet proposed by the Navy necessarily wrong. What could be wrong, however, is that the maritime

15. Ibid., pp. 33–34.
16. Ibid., pp. 35–36.

Table 2-1. Current U.S. Navy Force "Requirements"

Fleet	Peacetime maritime strategy[a]	Wartime maritime strategy
Sixth (Mediterranean)		
Carrier battle group	1.3	4
Battleship surface action group	0.3	1
Underway replenishment group	1.0	2
Second (Atlantic)[b]		
Carrier battle group	6.7	4
Battleship surface action group	1.7	1
Underway replenishment group	4.0	3
Seventh (Western Pacific)[c]		
Carrier battle group	2.0	5
Battleship surface action group	0.5	2
Underway replenishment group	1.0	4
Third[b]		
Carrier battle group	5.0	2
Battleship surface action group	1.5	. . .
Underway replenishment group	4.0	1
Total		
Carrier battle group	15	15
Battleship surface action group	4	4
Underway replenishment group	10	10

Source: Admiral James D. Watkins, U.S. Navy, *The Maritime Strategy* (Annapolis: U.S. Naval Institute, 1986), p. 36.

a. The fractions reflect average amounts of time spent in a particular fleet. Thus, on the average, there are 1.3 carrier battle groups in the Sixth Fleet in peacetime.

b. Includes forces in overhaul and training.

c. Includes forces rotated to the Indian Ocean.

strategy, with its substantial ambitions, is inconsistent with a navy of 600 ships, or 700 ships, or 800 ships.

Thus, in returning to the questions raised by the secretary of the navy, the United States does not have a serious strategic concept that can guide the planning and training of its naval forces. Consequently, we do not know whether the United States needs 600 ships or what should be their composition. Sir Edward Carson, when he became First Lord of the Admiralty in 1916, remarked, "My only great qualification for being put in charge of the Navy is that I am very much at sea." Readers of *The Maritime Strategy* will conclude their study of the document with much the same feeling. In the circumstances it becomes necessary once again to ask the question raised by the secretary of the navy: "Do we really need so many ships?"

CHAPTER THREE

THE NAVY AND THE
STRATEGIC NUCLEAR FORCES

ACCORDING to the current method used to measure the size of the Navy, its deployable battle forces include U.S. ballistic missile submarines (SSBNs) and their support ships. It may be well, therefore, to begin by asking what the size of that force should be. Secretary of the Navy Lehman begs the question by referring to "an adequate number of ballistic missile submarines,"[1] presumably on the ground that the total will result from a national rather than a Navy decision and will be determined by interservice and arms control considerations. However, because ballistic missile submarines possess such special characteristics, their number and composition deserve analysis independently of such considerations.

Strategic Nuclear Deterrence

Any approach to this issue should start with the recognition that the strategic nuclear forces have become capabilities of last resort. The reasons for that are almost too long to catalog. But at a time when more than 5,000 U.S. nuclear warheads are on the alert and ready for launch, when talk continues of impenetrable nuclear shields, surgical nuclear strikes, and protracted nuclear war, some of those reasons are worth recalling.

Deterrence is what everyone hopes these forces are all about. But deterrence contains the threat that, in the event of some transgression, nuclear weapons will be used against the transgressor. All this may seem

1. Admiral James D. Watkins, U.S. Navy, *The Maritime Strategy* (Annapolis: U.S. Naval Institute, 1986), pp. 35–36.

obvious, except that the planners who must design the strategic nuclear forces and develop the plans for executing the threat will sooner or later realize that it must possess some degree of credibility and acceptability if it is to have the desired deterrent effect. Hardly anyone would argue that the president of the United States, who has the sole legal authority in such matters, should release the alert strategic nuclear forces, or some portion of them, if a battalion of Soviet troops meandered across the interzonal border of Germany. The threat to destroy Soviet cities regardless of the provocation no longer has the ring of credibility. The idea of blowing up Nicaragua with a few nuclear weapons, while feasible, is simply unacceptable.

Credibility and acceptability, in short, are hard to come by when the threat to use nuclear weapons is at issue. Very small nuclear weapons may not cause much more damage than very large nonnuclear explosives, but the use of small nuclear weapons could lead to the use of larger nuclear weapons, and the effects of the exchanges could quickly become devastating. Historically, it has taken a great deal of time, effort, and expenditure to kill large numbers of soldiers and civilians, although World Wars I and II demonstrated that the art of mass destruction was improving, especially as attacks on civilians increased in frequency. Nuclear weapons have made the task easy. In the space of a few hours, if that is the objective, the United States and the Soviet Union, between them, can kill hundreds of millions of people. Even if that is not what they intend, it is difficult to visualize a large nuclear exchange between the two superpowers that would not result in tens of millions of prompt fatalities.[2] Although avoidance of cities and attacks on other targets may be preferable to the deliberate destruction of urban populations, the prospect of so many fatalities is not comforting or conducive to reckless behavior.

Ironically, nuclear weapons have stood history on its head. In the past, rules existed against attacking civilians, but the main concern was to obtain some major objective such as the unconditional surrender of Germany and Japan. Now the central issue confronting planners is whether or to what extent nuclear weapons can be used without rapidly producing a catastrophe of unprecedented proportions. None of the theories and none of the plans have yet come up with a satisfactory

2. See William Daugherty, Barbara Levi, and Frank von Hippel, "The Consequences of 'Limited' Nuclear Attacks on the United States," *International Security*, vol. 10 (Spring 1986), p. 35.

resolution. In principle, a full-scale, first-strike disarming attack that would eliminate an enemy's nuclear capabilities could limit the disaster on both sides and bring the war to a speedy and meaningful conclusion. Indeed, the capability for such an attack would probably be enough to deter a wide range of transgressions, although its acceptability as an instrument of U.S. policy might well remain in doubt. However, the Soviet Union is not now and never has been in a position to deliver such a knockout blow. The United States, if it ever was in such a position (an arguable matter), lost it more than twenty years ago.

A number of ways to substitute for the knockout blow have been invented in an effort to maintain or broaden the credibility of the strategic nuclear threat. All of them have proved complex, defective, and risky. Long before the introduction of the strategic defense initiative (more popularly known as Star Wars), the United States studied in some detail the possibility of what was known at the time as a damage-limiting strategy. In one version, it would, by a combination of offensive and defensive measures, attempt both to keep the fatalities from a nuclear exchange to relatively low levels and to disarm the enemy in the process. However, fear that implementation of the necessary programs would set off a costly and pointless duel of measures and countermeasures between the United States and the Soviet Union (as projected in table 3-1) led not only to the abandonment of the concept but also to growing opposition to the deployment of even a modest but expensive antiballistic missile defense ostensibly directed against China.

Other schemes followed. One was intended to ensure that the United States could recover more rapidly from a nuclear exchange than the Soviet Union. Another would have attempted to preserve a substantial U.S. offensive capability after one or more exchanges, while reducing the enemy offense to a small, essentially counter-city reserve. It was hoped that, from there, the United States could coerce the enemy into surrender by attacks on nonurban targets of value while maintaining a large counter-city reserve of its own.

All these approaches raise more questions than they answer. How would U.S. leaders know what they had accomplished, especially if key surveillance satellites had been taken out of action? What would happen if the enemy began to draw on his counter-city reserve to answer the U.S. coercive strikes? What are the chances that he might begin to attack U.S. cities in response to the coercion? And even supposing that he did none of these things, how would the process of terminating the exchanges and arranging the terms of surrender actually work? These questions,

Table 3-1. Number of Soviet and U.S. Fatalities in an All-Out Strategic Nuclear Exchange
Fatalities in millions[a]

U.S. action	Soviet action	Soviet first strike[b]		U.S. first strike[c]	
		U.S. fatalities	Soviet fatalities	U.S. fatalities	Soviet fatalities
Programmed force	Programmed force	120	120	120	80
Sentinel antiballistic missile defense added[d]	None	100	120	90	80
Same	Penetration aids added	120	120	110	80
Light defense of 25 cities added[e]	None	40	120	10	80
Same	Penetration aids, MIRVs, 100 mobile ICBMs added	110	120	90	80
Heavy defense of 52 cities (total) added[f]	None	20	120	10	80
Same	Penetration aids, MIRVs, 500 mobile ICBMs added	100	120	90	80

Source: *Department of Defense Annual Report, Fiscal Year 1969*, p. 64.
a. Exchange was assumed to occur in mid-1970s. U.S. population was estimated at 240 million, Soviet population at 270 million. Both sides proved less fertile.
b. The Soviet first strike attacked both military and urban targets; the U.S. retaliation attacked Soviet cities.
c. The U.S. first strike attacked military targets only; the Soviet second strike attacked urban targets only. Residual U.S. forces then attacked Soviet cities.
d. The Sentinel ABM system was intended to provide what is known as an area defense of the United States.
e. This ABM system consisted of a strengthened area defense and a point defense of 25 U.S. cities.
f. This ABM system consisted of a strengthened and more sophisticated area defense together with a thicker point defense of a total of 52 cities.

for which there are no satisfactory answers, make it doubtful that any of the current ideas would inspire sufficient confidence in the president to make him want to test its merits.

There are additional reasons why the strategic nuclear forces have become capabilities of last resort. As with other air and missile forces, they are limited in what they can do. They do not defend, seize, or occupy territory; they simply destroy targets. The result is that, short of a knockout blow, they are not good at creating or demonstrating a meaningful military advantage. No one can point at a map and say, "The strategic nuclear forces will capture Moscow in three days."

Furthermore, nuclear delivery systems are difficult to control even assuming their communications have not been knocked out. The problem with many of the launchers is that if they are not used rather quickly, they are likely to be destroyed. Admittedly, the pace of a nuclear conflict could be slower than is generally assumed. But many of the strikes are preprogrammed, and most of the command systems lack much endurance; they might well collapse before the complex process of ending a war could be completed. These limitations, combined with the taboo on the use of nuclear weapons that has lasted for more than forty years, restrict still further what can credibly be expected of the nuclear forces.

What, then, is left for them to do after all these years? If sensibly designed, they can certainly deter nuclear attacks on the United States. Perhaps less certainly, they can deter nuclear attacks on U.S. allies, in part because the Soviet leaders would have to consider that, in launching strikes against such an ally, they would leave themselves open to both allied responses and a full-scale attack by an undamaged U.S. strategic capability. Furthermore, the experience of the years since World War II suggests that, although the nuclear forces have not succeeded in deterring some conventional attacks—witness Korea and Vietnam— they have induced certain limits and elements of caution in the conduct of nonnuclear wars. And the chances are, despite the flamboyance of schemes such as the maritime strategy, that the strategic nuclear forces will continue to exercise the same kind of discipline on nonnuclear operations in the future.

Strategic Nuclear Objectives

Once it is recognized that those are the essential functions of the strategic nuclear forces, generally credible and acceptable goals for the forces are relatively easy to specify. First and foremost, the forces themselves must be made sufficiently survivable to make any potential attacker certain of their potential for major retaliation on a second strike. Second, the second-strike forces must have the capability of denying the attacker any meaningful and demonstrable advantage, and of inflicting heavy urban-industrial damage if the attacker should be tempted to strike at U.S. cities. Third, not only should options for the use of these forces exist, so that the president is not bound to a single response regardless of the nature of the attack, but the options, and the forces committed to them, should be so organized that opportunities to control and halt the exchanges become available.

None of these goals, it should be noted, addresses the issue of Soviet perceptions, even though, according to Secretary of Defense Weinberger, "an adversary's perceptions are an essential dimension of deterrence," whatever that may signify. But assuming that planners are attempting with U.S. strategic nuclear forces and plans to dissuade Soviet leaders from ordering various types of attacks, it is by no means clear how to affect their thinking on this score because of "our relative ignorance of Soviet perceptions," as the secretary himself confesses.[3] Indeed, talk about perceptions as an important factor in shaping the size and composition of U.S. nuclear or other forces is pointless unless the purpose is to avoid any objective criteria by which to measure the adequacy of those forces.

Pretending to relate U.S. capabilities to Soviet perceptions is especially pernicious when it comes to planning the U.S. strategic nuclear forces. Not only do planners lack data about Soviet perceptions, but they are not even sure whose perceptions they are trying to influence. The odds seem high, moreover, that such ignorance does not much matter. There is, after all, nothing subtle about what nuclear weapons can do. Consequently, if the strategic nuclear forces are conservatively planned, the necessary messages are likely to be conveyed to any potential attacker. That approach appears to have worked in the past, and short of an extraordinary transformation in the leadership of the Soviet Union or in the utility of nuclear weapons, it should work in the future.

At the heart of conservative force planning is a comprehensive target list that might contain 5,000 or more separate aiming points made up of missile silos, command centers, ballistic missile submarine ports, bomber bases, troop bases, tactical airfields, naval bases, transportation networks, energy sources, and industrial targets in cities. The strategic nuclear offense should be designed so that, on a second strike, it can attack the entire list (an example of which is in table 3-2) with a high probability of success. What constitutes an acceptable probability of kill should be, but usually is not, an issue for debate, because the size of the offensive force will be sensitive to this probability, particularly as it pertains to hard targets. The Air Force appears to be wedded to an 80

3. *Department of Defense Annual Report, Fiscal Year 1987,* p. 38.

Table 3-2. Hypothetical Target List for U.S. Strategic Nuclear Forces[a]

	Number of aiming points						
	Strategic nuclear forces		Peripheral attack forces[b]	General purpose forces	Logistics and energy	Urban-industrial	Total
Type of target	Hard	Soft					
ICBM silo	1,398	...	...	...	...	...	1,398
Launch control center	72	...	100	...	...	...	172
Nuclear storage site	100	...	...	...	...	...	100
National command center	100	...	...	...	...	...	100
Strategic nuclear submarine base	...	2	...	...	...	...	2
Heavy bomber base	...	50	...	...	...	...	50
Communication link	...	114	...	...	...	...	114
Radar	...	150	...	...	...	...	150
Medium-range, intermediate-range ballistic missile	...	...	600	...	...	...	600
Medium bomber base	...	...	40	...	...	...	40
Land forces base	...	...	...	200	...	...	200
Frontal aviation base	...	...	...	150	...	...	150
Fleet base	...	...	...	20	...	...	20
Higher headquarters (general purpose forces)	...	...	...	40	...	...	40
Transportation choke point	...	...	...	...	400	...	400
Energy source	...	...	...	...	100	...	100
Urban-industrial target							
Largest 10 cities	...	...	...	...	...	365	365
Next 40 largest cities	...	...	...	...	...	455	455
Next 50 largest cities	...	...	...	...	...	270	270
Next 100 largest cities	...	...	...	...	...	290	290
Total	1,670	316	740	410	500	1,380	5,016

Source: Author's estimates.

a. All targets are located in the Soviet Union.

b. The peripheral attack forces can reach targets in Europe, the Middle East, and Asia from launchers based in the USSR.

percent probability of kill against each target, hard or soft, on the long list contained in the Single Integrated Operational Plan (SIOP)—the war plan for the strategic nuclear forces and the basic threat with which any attacker must contend. However, there is no particular magic attached to this probability; depending on cost, it could plausibly be set higher or lower.

The ability of the U.S. strategic offense to cover a comprehensive target list on a second strike is only one test of its qualification as a credible and acceptable deterrent. The force should also be able to withhold attacks against one or more of the classes of targets included in the list. Thus if an enemy contemplated an attack in which the first echelon of missiles would attempt to destroy U.S. retaliatory forces, while subsequent echelons of missiles and bombers would be available for attacks on nonurban and city targets, he should be made to face the following prospect: that a portion of the U.S. offense could strike back at residual enemy forces; and that the remainder could be withheld to respond in kind should the attacker be in a position to launch coercive strikes or engage in a campaign of indiscriminate destruction.

Targets and Forces

The development of options obviously affects both the kinds of forces deployed by the United States and the targets assigned to them. If forces are to be withheld, they must have not only good chances of surviving an immediate attack, but also the endurance to remain available for launch after days or conceivably weeks. If a wide range of targets, including hard targets, is to be covered and, at the same time, unintended damage to the enemy is to be limited (unless he attacks cities), accurate and reliable delivery systems will continue to be in demand. Accuracy permits attacks on hard targets to be made with relative economy; it also allows nuclear yields to be substantially reduced for attacks on soft targets, thereby lessening the effects of excessive blast, heat, and radiation. Reliability means that fewer weapons have to be launched to obtain a high probability of destroying a particular target.

Policymakers have several key interests in target selection and weapons assignment. The first is that the targets themselves be chosen to achieve national objectives rather than force expansion. The second is that aiming points for nonurban targets be selected so as to minimize collateral damage to civilians. The third is that delivery systems with relatively poor survivability and endurance be allocated to targets that are almost certain to be attacked in the initial retaliation, regardless of how the enemy might design his first strike. The fourth is that targets whose destruction is unlikely to be urgent—transportation, energy, or industry, for example—be assigned to delivery systems with high survivability and endurance.

These kinds of allocations are especially important if the U.S. response is to be controlled. They help to prevent targets that the president might not want destroyed in an initial retaliation from being attacked simply because of a preference for launching certain delivery systems rather than losing them. Careful assignment of targets also helps to provide intervals between attacks during which, conceivably, the disaster could be brought to a halt. Thus, although it is debatable whether hard targets are as "time urgent" as many strategic planners assume, the odds are high that the president would want to order a major response to an enemy attack if for no other reason than to demonstrate that the enemy had not succeeded in delivering a knockout blow. Missile silos and bomber bases, for example, would constitute logical targets for this kind of demonstration. And intercontinental ballistic missiles (ICBMs) and bombers would be the logical delivery systems to assign to those targets. Since fixed, hard ICBMs are expected to have poor survivability, those surviving an initial attack would probably have to be launched without delay. Consequently, their preferred destination would be enemy missile silos.

Bombers are usually characterized as more controllable, but that is not really true. Bombers are not easy to protect on the ground; therefore, some of them are always kept on alert, ready to launch on warning of an attack. It is this part of the force that is considered survivable. If the alert bombers (usually 30 percent of the force in peacetime) were launched, they would proceed to their positive control line, at a northern latitude, where they would loiter, or return to their bases, unless given a positive and authenticated order to cross the line and proceed to their targets. Suppose that 90 bombers with some 720 nuclear weapons on board had flown to the positive control line. It seems probable that the entire force would either return to base (perhaps because of a false alarm) or be committed to the initial retaliation. It would be difficult, in the latter eventuality, to call a raid of this size limited or surgical. And the force would probably be within about four hours of its assigned targets, on the average—an interval of sorts for stopping the exchange, but not much of one. In these circumstances it is doubtful that the president would want the raid committed to nonurgent targets or such targets of last resort as cities. Hence it makes sense to allocate the bombers as well as the ICBMs to enemy strategic forces and to peripheral attack forces (those directly threatening U.S. allies).

The Navy's Role

So far so good, but what has all this got to do with the United States Navy? A great deal, as it turns out, for the Navy, with its ballistic missile submarines, is capable of meeting most of the conditions set by what has been called the countervailing strategy. Although some people are horrified by the idea that Admiral Watkins would like to sink Soviet SSBNs during a conventional war, they overlook the fact that Soviet antisubmarine warfare capabilities appear to be devoted principally to the sinking of U.S. SSBNs. So far, however, that dedication does not seem likely to enjoy much chance of success. The submarine leg of the strategic nuclear Triad (the other two legs consisting of ICBMs and bombers) is by far the most survivable of the three, and that attribute is likely to last for the foreseeable future. U.S. SSBNs also have superior endurance: between 55 percent and 65 percent of them are on patrol and within range of their targets at all times, and their patrols can last for 70 days or longer. In a crisis, even more of them could go out on station, perhaps as many as 80 percent.

What is more, with the introduction of the Trident I (C-4) ballistic missile, the SSBNs can patrol in larger areas of the oceans, cover more targets, and achieve responses as rapid as those of ICBMs against time-urgent targets. Once the Trident II (D-5) missile is deployed—with production scheduled to begin in 1987 and deployment in 1989—the submarine-launched ballistic missile (SLBM) will compete favorably with the Minuteman III (Mark 12A) and the MX ICBMs in accuracy, although its probability of kill against hard targets may be lower, depending on the yields of its multiple independently targetable reentry vehicles (MIRVs). In short, SLBMs will soon have the capability to cover all the hard and soft targets on the U.S. target list. Furthermore, because of their enduring survivability, missiles aboard SSBNs can be withheld for substantial periods of time, thereby providing those intervals during which it might prove possible to halt the exchanges. And insofar as a postwar nuclear reserve might be useful, the SSBNs can provide it either from the forces withheld from attacking cities (if, as is to be hoped, they are not used), or from the submarines that would be in transit between their home posts and wartime stations—as much as 20 percent of the force.

The SSBNs possess one other important advantage, that of cost. True, the latest Trident-class submarine costs about $1.7 billion, and each of its 24 D-5 missiles is currently priced at $40 million. Moreover, its operating cost runs high compared with that of an ICBM in a fixed, hard silo, though not with that of a bomber or a land-mobile missile such as the small ICBM (or Midgetman). But if the investment and operating costs of all these systems are allocated to the number of warheads delivered to targets on a second strike, the Trident beats them all, even though no more than 65 percent of the boats and missiles would be on station and ready to fire during a peacetime day-to-day alert.

Force Mixes

With all these advantages, why does the United States not forgo ICBMs and bombers and rely exclusively on SLBMs for its countervailing force? One argument against doing so is the difficulty of communicating reliably and securely with the SSBNs at all times. Critics have probably exaggerated this weakness, especially since in most instances the entire offensive force—whether ICBMs, bombers, or SLBMs—will have to rely on airborne communications for their orders. Perhaps a more serious problem is that the Air Force would fiercely resist its exclusion from the strategic role, and the Navy itself would worry about the SSBNs gobbling up too much of its share of the budget pie.

In a less parochial vein, there remains the traditional and homely issue of how many strategic eggs the United States should put in one basket. More specifically, it is conceivable that ways will be found in the future to maintain a track on all the SSBNs at sea and destroy them simultaneously. Alternatively, just as Admiral Watkins would like to erode or eliminate the Soviet SLBM force during a conventional war at sea, so the Russians might try to destroy U.S. SSBNs under similar conditions, and without escalation. It is also possible—though less so than was thought in the past—that a great majority of the SSBNs could suffer a massive failure in an attempt to launch under stress. Finally, if the United States were to concentrate all its strategic resources on one offensive weapon, that would facilitate a similar concentration of Soviet resources on countermeasures to it. As matters now stand, Soviet planners must worry about aerodynamic vehicles coming in at low altitudes, ICBMs approaching on polar trajectories, and SLBMs attacking from the Atlantic and Pacific as well as from other locations.

As long as it is cheaper for the United States to maintain the diversity of the Triad than it is for the Soviet Union to counter it, the case for the Triad remains strong. However, doubts are warranted about whether the United States is maintaining a favorable cost-exchange ratio in this tragic rivalry with the Soviet Union. The country has already paid a heavy price for the MX, an ICBM rated as having a low probability of surviving a Soviet first strike, and it is now engaged in an expensive gamble on the Midgetman, a relatively small land-mobile ICBM that may prove no more survivable than the MX. Although the U.S. bomber force has probably exerted tremendous leverage on the Soviet Union by causing it to make a massive and disproportionate investment in air defenses, that leverage is being frittered away by the insistence of the Defense Department (despite its alleged loyalty to "competitive strategies") on producing two very expensive penetrating bombers—the B-1B and the Stealth, or advanced technology bomber (ATB)—which will duplicate the functions that long-range cruise missiles can already perform at a much lower price. The time may not yet have arrived to abandon the Triad, but these developments make clear that the time is past due to question whether the emphasis on the three legs of the Triad should not change.

A New Look

Current U.S. strategic nuclear offensive forces and their estimated annual costs (in 1987 dollars) are shown in table 3-3. The bombers and their refueling tankers constitute the most expensive part of the offense, the SLBMs come next, and the ICBMs are the cheapest. The SLBMs, however, are the cheapest per second-strike delivered warhead, while the ICBMs—because they would suffer such heavy losses from a Soviet first strike—are by this measure among the most expensive. To put it another way, SLBMs have a very high output for their cost, whereas the ICBMs have a very low output for their cost.

Suppose for a moment that SALT II constraints were still in effect. Suppose further that the target list for the U.S. offense consisted of the aiming points provided in table 3-2 and that an overall damage expectancy of 70 percent were desired against the target list. What might be the most efficient U.S. offensive force during the coming decade consistent with maintaining the Triad?

There is no obviously right answer to this question, but several guides exist to the design of such a force. One guide is presented in table 3-4, which estimates the acquisition cost per second-strike delivered warhead for various delivery systems. These estimates are based on two main assumptions: that by the early 1990s the Soviet Union will obtain the

Table 3-3. U.S. Strategic Nuclear Forces and Their Costs, Fiscal Year 1987
Costs in billions of fiscal 1987 dollars

System	Number	Annual investment, operating, and support cost
Strategic bombers[a]		
B-52G (with cruise missiles)	138	6.2
B-52H	96	3.6
FB-111	52	1.9
B-1B	60	5.1
KC-135 refueling aircraft	600	6.4
Subtotal	. . .	23.2
Land-based ICBMs		
Titan II	2	0.1
Minuteman II	450	2.5
Minuteman III	513	3.3
MX	27	1.6
Subtotal	. . .	7.5
Fleet ballistic launchers (SLBMs)		
Poseidon/C-3 (Poseidon missile)	144	2.7
Poseidon/C-4 (Trident I missile)	192	3.6
Trident/C-4 (Trident I missile)	192	4.4
Subtotal	. . .	10.7
Strategic defense		
Interceptors[a]	249	1.9
Strategic defense initiative	. . .	4.8
Subtotal	. . .	6.7
Early warning, command, control, and communications	. . .	4.8
Subtotal	. . .	4.8
Total	. . .	52.9[b]

Sources: *Department of Defense Annual Report, Fiscal Year 1987,* table 1, app. C, p. 323; and author's estimates.

a. Primary authorized aircraft (PAA), which do not include aircraft for training or attrition or in mothballs.

b. The total is less than shown in table 5-1 because it does not include a share of program III (national intelligence and communications). The amount reflects the administration's request rather than final congressional action on the fiscal 1987 defense budget.

necessary combination of accuracy, warhead yield, and reliability in its ICBM force to destroy 96 percent of U.S. ICBM silos; and that it will deploy a first-generation look-down, shoot-down air defense system comparable to what the United States has had for some time in the form of the AWACS (airborne warning and control system) aircraft and the F-15 fighter. A second guide arises from the desirability of retaining an ICBM force large enough to prevent, at a minimum, Soviet planners from ignoring it. It would thereby facilitate the survival of the alert bombers or, if an effort were made to catch the alert bombers before they escaped, would permit the launch of an undamaged ICBM force.

Based on these considerations, it clearly makes sense to emphasize the SLBM leg of the Triad. The United States at present (1986) deploys 16 older Poseidon boats, each with 16 Poseidon missiles; 12 newer Poseidon SSBNs, each with 16 Trident I missiles; and 8 Trident boats, each with 24 Trident I missiles. In all, these 36 SSBNs provide a total of 604 SLBMs and about 5,632 warheads. Since Congress has already funded 5 more Trident boats that have not yet been delivered, the number of SLBMs could keep rising (depending on decisions about decommissioning some of the older Poseidon SSBNs). And between 1986 and 1992 another 6 Trident boats could manageably be funded even within tight defense budget constraints. Consequently, it would be feasible, and certainly desirable, to deploy an SLBM force in the late 1990s consisting of 41 SSBNs (19 Tridents and 22 Poseidons), 808 launchers, and about 6,784 warheads (see table 3-5).

The data contained in table 3-4 strongly suggest that it makes sense to maintain the 120 cruise-missile-carrying bombers originally contemplated in the SALT II agreement and to use B-1Bs as the carriers. Assuming SALT II constraints of 1,200 MIRVed ballistic missiles, that would leave an allowable force of 392 ICBMs, of which 50 would be MX (with 500 warheads). The remaining 342 would consist of the Minuteman III, all modified to carry the Mark 12A front end (with 1,026 warheads). In all, the ICBMs would contain 1,526 warheads, more than enough, surely, to force a Soviet attack on them in a first strike. Thus if the alert bombers escaped, they would carry more than 1,000 cruise missiles; if the alert ICBMs escaped, they would launch nearly 1,400 warheads. Furthermore, since approximately 24 SSBNs would be on station at all times with 3,600 or more warheads, and another 9 might be in port, as many as 8 with more than 1,300 warheads would be in training or transit and available as a postwar reserve.

Measuring Performance

Although this new look would provide the strategic offense with only 1,320 launchers (bombers as well as missiles), well below the thirty-year

Table 3-4. Acquisition Cost per Second-Strike Deliverable Warhead[a]
Costs in millions of fiscal 1987 dollars

System	Number	Warheads	Alert rate	Probability of alert warheads surviving	Reliability	Penetration probability[b]	Cost per delivered warhead[c]
Strategic bombers							
B-52G (with cruise missiles)	138	1,656	.3	.3	.8	.98[d]	74
B-52H	96	768	.3	.3	.8	.06	1,500
FB-111	52	312	.3	.3	.8	.06	2,000
B-1B	100	1,200	.3	.3	.8	.22	464
B-1B[e]	100	1,200	.5	.5	.8	.41	200
Advanced technology bomber (Stealth)	132	1,320	.3	.3	.8	.53	268
Advanced technology bomber (Stealth)[e]	132	1,320	.5	.5	.8	.68	166
Land-based ICBMs							
Minuteman II	450	450	.9	.036	.8	1.0	1,219
Minuteman III	500	1,500	.9	.036	.8	1.0	463
MX	50	500	.9	.036	.8	1.0	854
Small ICBM (mobile Midgetman)[f]	500	1,000	.9	.27	.8	1.0	208
Small ICBM (mobile Midgetman)[f]	500	1,000	.9	.45	.8	1.0	125
Small ICBM (mobile Midgetman)[f]	500	1,000	.9	.72	.8	1.0	78
Fleet ballistic launchers (SLBMs)							
Poseidon/C-3 (Poseidon missile)	160	1,600	.495	.495	.8	1.0	23
Poseidon/C-4 (Trident I missile)	192	1,536	.54	.54	.8	1.0	29
Trident/C-4 (Trident I missile)	192	1,536	.54	.54	.8	1.0	35
Trident/D-5 (Trident II missile)	264	2,112	.54	.54	.8	1.0	50

Source: Author's estimates.

a. A second-strike deliverable warhead is defined here as a warhead that survives a Soviet surprise attack, launches, penetrates any defenses, and lands in the Soviet Union.

b. Bomber penetration probabilities are based on the assumption that the USSR has deployed a look-down, shoot-down air defense system comparable to a first-generation AWACS (airborne warning and control system)–F-15 combination.

c. Cost per delivered warhead is calculated as the acquisition cost of the warheads and their launchers divided by the number of second-strike delivered warheads. Adding operating and support costs (including tanker support for the bombers) would make the ICBMs (except for Midgetman) look somewhat less costly relative to the bombers, but would not significantly reduce the cost advantage of the SLBMs.

d. The bombers do not penetrate; only the cruise missiles do.

e. These examples show the utility of higher alert rates. Cruise missile carriers would benefit similarly despite the cost of additional crews and maintenance.

f. These examples reflect the large uncertainty about the survivability of Midgetman. The ''congressional'' missile would have only one warhead.

Table 3-5. U.S. Submarine-Launched Ballistic Missile Force in Fiscal Year 1986 and Feasible SLBM Capability in Fiscal Year 1997

Year and component	*Ballistic missile submarine class*					
	Lafayette	*Madison and Franklin*	*Madison and Franklin*	*Ohio*	*Ohio*	*Total*
Fiscal 1986						
Submarines	6	10	12	8	. . .	36
Launchers	96	160	192	192	. . .	640
Missile	C-3	C-3	C-4	C-4	. . .	. . .
Warheads	960	1,600	1,536	1,536	. . .	5,632
Fiscal 1997[a]						
Submarines	. . .	10	12	8	11	41
Launchers	. . .	160	192	192	264	2,112
Missile	. . .	C-3	C-4	C-4	D-5	. . .
Warheads	. . .	1,600	1,536	1,536	2,112	6,784

Sources: *Department of Defense Annual Report, Fiscal Year 1987*, table 1, app. C, p. 323; John M. Collins, *U.S.-Soviet Military Balance, 1980–1985* (Washington, D.C.: Pergamon Brassey's, 1985), pp. 176–78; and author's estimates.

a. The fiscal 1997 force is based on the following assumptions: that the Madison and Franklin classes held in the force are those commissioned in 1965 or later; that 13 Ohio-class submarines have been funded through fiscal 1986; and that another 6 Ohio-class submarines will be funded between fiscal 1987 and fiscal 1992. Therefore, 19 Ohio-class submarines should be in service by fiscal 1997.

average of 2,000, it would give the United States an extremely powerful deterrent. As estimated, this so-called efficient force, even after a well-executed Soviet first strike, would be able—from a regular day-to-day alert—to deliver more than 3,700 warheads to targets in the Soviet Union in what is known as a laydown, in which all surviving alert delivery systems are assumed to have been launched (see table 3-6). On the average, this hypothetical retaliation would destroy 75 percent of its targets. Prompt fatalities from attacks on Soviet cities would amount to 80 million, or 30 percent of the total population. Fatalities resulting from attacks on nonurban targets would reach 14 million, or 5 percent of the total population.

As table 3-6 also shows, the results would be even more horrendous if the U.S. strategic forces were on a generated alert—as they were during the Cuban missile crisis—a more likely eventuality than a day-to-day alert, since a Soviet first strike would probably receive somewhat more serious consideration in a great crisis than in more peaceable times. Indeed, it is doubtful that either Mikhail S. Gorbachev or Ronald Reagan checks each noncrisis day to see whether the propitious moment has arrived to launch a surprise attack.

Table 3-6. Performance of the Efficient Strategic Nuclear Force after a Soviet First Strike

System	Warheads	Alert, surviving warheads	Allocation of alert, surviving weapons						Total targets
			Hard strategic targets	Soft strategic targets	Peripheral attack targets	General purpose forces targets	Logistical and energy targets	Urban industrial aiming points	
Day-to-day alert									
120 B-1B bombers	3,360	1,008	1,008	...	...	...	...	...	1,008
50 MX ICBMs	500	18	18	...	...	...	...	...	18
342 Minuteman III ICBMs	1,026	37	37	...	...	...	...	...	37
160 Poseidon/C-3 SLBMs	1,600	792	...	...	575	...	...	792	792
192 Poseidon/C-4 SLBMs	1,536	829	...	...	575	...	254	...	829
192 Trident/C-4 SLBMs	1,536	912	...	...	...	78	246	588	912
264 Trident/D-5 SLBMs	2,112	1,255	607	316	...	332	...	...	1,255
All weapons	11,670	4,851	1,670	316	575	410	500	1,380	4,851
Weapons delivered	...	...	1,322	253	460	328	400	1,054[a]	3,817
Targets destroyed	...	...	1,251	253	460	328	400	1,054	3,746
Damage expectancy[a]	...	...	74.9	80.0	62.0	80.0	80.0	76.4	74.7
Generated alert									
120 B-1B bombers	3,360	2,688	2,688	...	...	...	...	...	2,688
50 MX ICBMs	500	18	18	...	...	...	...	...	18
342 Minuteman III ICBMs	1,026	37	37	...	...	...	...	...	37
160 Poseidon/C-3 SLBMs	1,600	1,152	...	...	...	...	...	1,152	1,152
192 Poseidon/C-3 SLBMs	1,536	1,106	...	...	405	410	...	291	1,106
192 Trident/C-4 SLBMs	1,536	1,106	...	606	...	...	500	...	1,106
264 Trident/C-4 SLBMs	2,112	1,521	597	26	335	63	500	...	1,521
All weapons	11,670	7,628	3,340	632	740	473	1,000	1,443	7,628
Weapons delivered	...	...	2,612	506	592	378	800	1,104[b]	5,992
Targets destroyed	...	...	1,573	303	592	338	480	1,104	4,390
Damage expectancy[a]	...	...	94.2	95.9	80.0	82.4	96.0	80.0	87.5

Sources: Tables 3-2, 3-5; and author's estimates.
a. Percent of targets destroyed.
b. It is assumed that the Moscow ABM system destroys 50 entering warheads.

Table 3-7. Cost of the Efficient Strategic Nuclear Forces, Fiscal Years 1987–97
Billions of 1987 dollars

Year	Strategic bombers	Land- based ICBMs	Fleet ballistic launch- ers (SLBMs)	Strategic defense	Early warning, com- mand, control, and com- munica- tions	Total
1987[a]	23.2	7.5	10.7	6.7	4.8	52.9[a]
1988	19.9	6.2	11.2	3.9	4.6	45.8
1989	18.7	5.8	11.8	3.9	4.5	44.7
1990	17.4	5.4	12.3	3.9	4.3	43.3
1991	16.2	5.1	12.8	3.9	4.1	42.1
1992	14.9	4.7	13.4	3.9	4.0	40.9
1993	13.6	4.4	13.9	3.9	3.8	39.6
1994	13.4	4.0	14.4	3.9	3.7	39.4
1995	12.1	4.0	14.9	3.9	3.6	38.5
1996	10.9	4.0	15.5	3.9	3.4	37.7
1997	10.6	3.9	16.0	3.9	3.3	37.7

Sources: Tables 3-3, 10-2; and author's estimates.
a. Reflects the administration's request rather than final congressional action on the fiscal 1987 defense budget.

Measuring Costs and Benefits

A strategic force with 1,320 offensive launchers, of which SSBNs would constitute the dominant component, would cause a net decline in that part of the defense budget devoted to the strategic deterrent during the coming decade. Trident boats would continue to be funded at a rate of one a year; the Trident II (D-5) missile would remain at the currently programmed pace; the residual Minuteman ICBMs would undergo modernization; and the B-1B would be converted to a cruise missile launcher. However, any real budgetary increases caused by these programs could be more than offset by the phasedown of the B-52 and FB-111 bombers, the cutback in Minuteman ICBMs, the termination of the MX, the decommissioning of older Poseidon boats for the strategic role, and a slower pace in such programs as the strategic defense initiative, Midgetman, and Stealth, for which no real demand would exist (see table 3-7).

Policymakers entranced with the will-o'-the-wisp of perceptions, worried about any disparity between U.S. and Soviet launchers and warheads, or persuaded that ICBMs with single warheads (regardless of the number of launchers and their cost) are less tempting targets than

MIRVed systems may balk at changing direction to this degree. Before they reject such a change, however, they may wish to take several other considerations into account.

It may make sense to retire the last six Lafayette-class SSBNs with their Poseidon (C-3) missiles as more Trident boats are commissioned. But there will remain 22 SSBNs of the James Madison and Benjamin Franklin classes that were deployed as late as 1965. Of these 22 boats, 12 carry the Trident I (C-4) missile and 10 the Poseidon (C-3) missile. None of these boats should need major rework or decommissioning until the 1990s. Consequently, whether the United States decides to go above or below the SALT II limits on MIRVed ballistic missiles, it makes far more sense to cut back on Minuteman IIIs (despite their low operating costs) than to keep trading Poseidon boats for Tridents.

The submarine-based force is substantially more cost effective than the Minuteman III when the two are properly compared. It should be evident, furthermore, that the United States holds a large comparative advantage over the Soviet Union in SSBNs, largely because of technology and geography. By contrast, the Soviet Union probably has some advantage over the United States in land-mobile missiles, primarily because of greater freedom over where and how to operate them. Rather than inhibit these developments, arms control should encourage them.

It is also well to recall under what conditions MIRVed missiles are a cause for alarm. There are two. The first is when they force the launching of more warheads than are called for by an option or a target set. The second is when the MIRVed missiles are both costly and vulnerable, since an enemy then has the potential to kill many valuable warheads with only one or two of his own. Despite much talk about limited options and surgical strikes (which rarely includes consideration of improved fuzing for the warheads or reduced fission-fusion ratios, both of which would help to limit damage), the first condition is not likely to arise even though the Navy expects to launch its SLBMs by the boatload and in a short period of time. As to the second condition, policymakers may wish to ask whether they are opposed to MIRVed missiles in general or only to expensive and vulnerable MIRVed missiles such as MX. If the former, they should oppose even the efficient Navy SLBM programs. If the latter, they should press for expanding the SLBM leg of the Triad. At the same time, they should question the worth of proceeding with a single-warhead, land-mobile ICBM that, by all estimates, will prove extremely costly but will mimic only poorly the qualities of the SSBN.

Table 3-8. Effectiveness and Cost of Capabilities Incremental to the Efficient Strategic Nuclear Forces[a]
Costs in billions of fiscal 1987 dollars

Item	Number	Warheads	Alert, surviving warheads	Delivered warheads	Annual investment, operating, and support cost
Incremental capability					
B-52 bombers	96	768	230[b]	12	3.1
Stealth bombers	132	1,320	396[b]	168	8.1
Minuteman II ICBMs	450	450	16[c]	13	2.4
Minuteman III ICBMs	158	474	17[c]	14	0.9
Small ICBMs (Midgetman)	450	900	405[d]	324	9.0
Total	1,286	3,912	1,064	531	23.5
Efficient force	1,320	11,670	4,851	3,817	37.7
Incremental cost-effectiveness (percent)	...	...	...	13.2	62.3

Sources: Tables 3-4, 3-6; and author's estimates.
a. Assumes a Soviet surprise attack and a U.S. second-strike retaliation from day-to-day alert.
b. 30 percent alert and surviving.
c. 90 percent alert and 4 percent surviving.
d. An optimistic case: 2 warheads per missile, 90 percent alert and dispersed, 50 percent surviving.

If relative numbers are important for perceptions, or alleged to be important, it would of course be possible to retain the B-52 and FB-111 bombers and all the Minuteman ICBMs in the strategic forces for many more years, and even to add both the Stealth bomber and some version of the small ICBM. Certainly they would help to preserve at least an artificial appearance of equality with the Soviet Union and might conceivably serve as bargaining chips in the strategic arms limitation talks, though probably not to the extent that used cars do in other types of trades. At some point, however, an end should come to the casual use of taxpayers' dollars for functions whose utility has yet to be demonstrated.

As table 3-8 shows, only 13 of the 450 Minuteman II warheads and 14 Minuteman III warheads could be expected to reach their targets on a second strike. Penetrating bombers would do somewhat better, but their operating costs are much greater. Overall, retention of these forces would add perhaps 13 percent to the number of delivered warheads on a second strike at an annual cost (in 1987 dollars) of approximately $23.5 billion. This small increment of damage—which would increase overall damage expectancy against the target list by 4.3 percent—hardly seems worth the cost.

In sum, the Navy has a superior product in the form of the Trident submarine and the C-4 and D-5 ballistic missiles. Arguments can be made that a smaller submarine with fewer missiles would make a less tempting and less detectable target. But pending resolution of that difficult issue, policymakers could do a lot worse than make the SLBMs the backbone of the U.S. strategic offensive forces.

CHAPTER FOUR

THE NAVY AND THE
TACTICAL NUCLEAR CAPABILITIES

IT IS no great secret, despite long-standing declaratory policy, that past U.S. presidents have harbored the gravest possible reservations about the wisdom of using the strategic nuclear forces in response to a conventional attack on allies. Had that not been the case, nuclear weapons and theater-based launchers would hardly have been deployed to Europe and Asia and on a variety of naval vessels, including aircraft carriers, surface combatants, and submarines. In 1983 the *New York Times* published an estimate of the stockpile of nuclear weapons for tactical use by type, number, and general location as it allegedly existed in that year (see table 4-1). Since then, the United States and its allies have agreed to the withdrawal of 1,400 of these weapons from Europe. Furthermore, as the United States deploys the intermediate-range Pershing II ballistic missile to Europe (along with 464 ground-launched cruise missiles and 116 launchers), it will presumably withdraw its shorter-range Pershing I missiles and warheads on a one-for-one basis.

Tactical Nuclear Illusions

An even greater number of illusions persist about these weapons than about the strategic nuclear forces. It is common, for example, to talk about tactical nuclear weapons and tactical nuclear forces, but neither actually exists. It is true that some nuclear weapons have yields measured in tons rather than kilotons and megatons, but low-yield weapons can be used against strategic targets and high-yield weapons against tactical targets. Nuclear weapons can be delivered from cannon, rockets, surface-to-air missiles, air-to-air missiles, tactical aircraft, torpedoes, and depth charges as well as from ballistic missiles and bombers. But

Table 4-1. U.S. Nuclear Stockpile for Tactical Nuclear Warfare

		In Europe				
		For				
	In the	For	non-	In the		
	United	U.S.	U.S.	Pacific		
Type of weapon	States	forces	forces	area	At sea	Total
Land-based						
Aircraft bombs	1,210	1,415	320	135	. . .	3,080
Pershing I missiles	. . .	195[a]	100	. . .	. . .	295
8-inch howitzers	200	505	430	65	. . .	1,200
155-mm howitzers	160	595	140	30	. . .	925
Lance missiles	210	325	370	. . .	. . .	905
Honest John rockets	100	. . .	200	. . .	. . .	300
Nike-Hercules surface-to-air missiles	55	300	390	. . .	. . .	745
Atomic demolition munitions	215	370	. . .	20	. . .	605
Naval						
Aircraft bombs	. . .	. . .	. . .	. . .	720	720
Depth charges	560	190	. . .	100	45	895
Terrier surface-to-air missiles	155	. . .	. . .	. . .	135	290
Antisubmarine rockets	225	. . .	. . .	. . .	350	575
Submarine rockets	110	. . .	. . .	. . .	175	285
Total	3,200	3,895[b]	1,950[b]	350	1,425	10,820

Source: Richard Halloran, "Report to Congress Provides Figures for Nuclear Arsenal," *New York Times,* November 15, 1983.

a. Warheads for the Pershing II, a longer-range missile, will replace some or all of these weapons.

b. Approximately 1,400 of these weapons have been or will be withdrawn from Europe.

there is no law against using B-52 heavy bombers or Minuteman ICBMs against targets in Eastern Europe, or refueled tactical fighters against targets in the Soviet Union. F-111s, which are nuclear capable, flew a total of approximately 5,400 miles in their bombing raids on Libya in 1986.

Most of the delivery systems the United States has deployed overseas, however, have relatively short ranges and are intended for attacks on tactical targets—that is, targets whose destruction would affect a land-air battle in the near term. These systems, for better or worse, are not organized into a separate nuclear command, nor can they be considered a specialized and dedicated force on the model of the Strategic Air Command. With the possible exception of the Pershing IIs and the ground-launched cruise missiles (GLCMs), they are part of what are called the general purpose forces: Army ground and helicopter units, Marine Corps divisions and associated air wings, Navy ships and attack submarines, and Air Force tactical fighter-attack wings. Many of the launchers, in fact, are dual purpose: they are designed so that they can fire either nuclear or conventional ordnance.

This jumbled capability deployed by the United States and many of its allies (but with most of their warheads under U.S. control) had its origins in the unique conditions of the late 1940s. At that time the Soviet Union deployed allegedly massive conventional forces but had no nuclear weapons (its first nuclear device was detonated in August 1949), whereas the United States possessed a small stockpile of nuclear weapons and an even smaller number of divisions and tactical air wings. Even with the formation of the North Atlantic Treaty Organization (NATO) in the spring of 1949, allied conventional forces in Europe were deemed incapable of stopping a Soviet drive to the English Channel. At this point nuclear weapons appeared as the *deus ex machina* of the alliance. The advocates of their deployment made several arguments that seemed compelling at the time: that Soviet forces would have to concentrate to break through NATO's defenses, paper thin though they were; that the tactical use of nuclear weapons could literally blow away these concentrations; and that relatively low yield nuclear weapons could therefore substitute for the additional conventional forces that the war-weary allies were unwilling to provide for a solid defense of Western Europe. With this substitution, not only would NATO have the means to defeat the Red hordes, and thereby deter them from attacking in the first place, but nuclear weapons would enable the alliance to obtain its deterrent on the cheap, both economically and politically. Thus was born the view that a free lunch did indeed exist and that it would exist forever and ever, because the first use of nuclear weapons would always redound to the advantage of the defense. Perhaps only a Jean Renoir could have done justice to the illusion.

The acquisition by the Soviet Union of a growing number of nuclear delivery systems, from short-range Frog rockets to medium bombers and intermediate-range ballistic missiles, should have undermined the original doctrine about the advantages or even the probability of NATO first use. On the surface, at least, it did not. Fears of the Red hordes continued unabated, despite mounting evidence that a stout allied defense was well within reach and would not prove too costly.

It did become evident to some that the Soviet Union, too, could use nuclear weapons and might well decide to fire them first (despite its explicit rejection of such a policy), doing perhaps fatal damage to vulnerable NATO defenses, including a large number of its short-range launchers and exposed tactical aircraft. Even so, most U.S. and allied military planners continued to cling to the old beliefs. In doing so, they indulged themselves in several new illusions: about the ability of the allies in concert to get the jump on the Warsaw Pact in making this crushing and unprecedented nuclear decision; about the prospect that NATO could fight a war of maneuver for some days or weeks in a nuclear environment—and, with its large and growing stockpile of low-yield nuclear weapons, outshoot and decimate the Warsaw Pact ground forces; about the feasibility of "clean" and limited nuclear campaigns fought with enhanced radiation weapons (otherwise known as neutron bombs), despite the arsenal of "dirty" medium-range nuclear missiles and bombers staring down the allies' throats from Soviet soil; about the advantages of a relatively small scale nuclear demonstration that would blow up a Soviet regiment or two and so frighten Soviet leaders (but not NATO statesmen and their populations) that they would stop whatever they were doing and return to wherever they had come from.

The Utility of Tactical Nuclear Capabilities

Although none of these allegations has particularly persuaded anyone but the allegators, there is a persuasive case for maintaining and improving U.S. tactical nuclear capabilities. Whatever the history of these capabilities and of the interaction between the great powers, the inescapable fact remains that the Soviet Union has deployed a remarkable array of nuclear delivery systems as a threat to every nation on its borders. De Gaulle may have preached the virtues of what he called an all-azimuth defense; the Soviet leadership has practiced them.

Moreover, despite the Soviet declaratory policy of no first use, it is as likely that the Soviet Union would fall into desperate military or political straits and violate its pledge as that the United States, Britain, or France would be the first to fire nuclear weapons in combat. To complicate matters even more, Soviet planners have indicated that during a conventional campaign of the kind that might be anticipated in Europe, they would seek to destroy as many NATO nuclear launchers as possible by means of nonnuclear attacks. For all these reasons, NATO should have a rather keen interest in tactical nuclear capabilities with good second-strike retaliatory power. But what might be the targets for retaliation?

Should the Soviet Union attack with nuclear weapons in an area as small and crowded as Western Europe, it could, for all practical purposes, blow up the entire region. Similarly, it could devastate Pakistan, India, South Korea, Japan, and for that matter the United States, just as the United States could lay waste to the Soviet Union. Indeed, that is likely to remain more or less the prospect whether each side deploys 20,000, 10,000, 5,000, or 1,000 thermonuclear weapons, depending on their yields. But unless the Soviets, like the Romans, have as their motto *delenda est Carthago,* they would surely want to use nuclear weapons to subdue rather than destroy their neighbors, and get rid of the American presence in the process.

Second-strike tactical nuclear capabilities may not suffice to prevent the Carthaginian solution. If properly designed, however, they can help to deter the second contingency and conceivably contribute to preventing any kind of attack on an area as important and sensitive as Western Europe, Korea, or Japan. Like the strategic nuclear forces, they too are bound to cast a shadow over any kind of confrontation regardless of the declaratory policy that accompanies them. But for force planning purposes, their sole military mission remains the deterrence of nuclear strikes by Soviet theater attack forces aimed at paving the way for the seizure and subjugation of U.S. allies and the isolation of the United States.

Force Planning

U.S. force planners need to take a number of steps to be confident of executing that mission. First and foremost, they should forget about U.S. declaratory policy, whether it is first use or no first use of nuclear weapons, and ensure that the president has a survivable, second-strike capability at his disposal. Not only is such a capability a matter of elementary prudence, given all the uncertainty over who might fire first; it also provides a higher probability that the president will be able to use nuclear weapons when they really need to be used—in retaliation.

Nuclear weapons have never been accepted as part of the peculiar culture of warfare; they are even more horrifying and even less likely to serve as rational means to national ends than biological or chemical weapons are. The demand to initiate their use forces the president to contemplate a range of uncertainty bounded at one end by the possibility of national disaster and at the other by a temporary victory wrapped in international obloquy. The burden of releasing nuclear weapons under these conditions is virtually intolerable. By contrast, if someone else has borne the burden and taken the risk, the decision to strike back approaches the realm of acceptable behavior. The president has every right to insist on that option.

Planners designing second-strike capabilities also owe it to the president to provide him with a range of possible responses to an enemy first use. In doing so, they need to abandon the view that a tactical nuclear campaign is an extension of traditional warfare with firepower sufficiently enhanced to favor the defense but not the offense. Because of their efficiency and the large range of yields they provide, nuclear weapons can rapidly destroy troop concentrations, miles of front, airfields, bridges, tunnels, command bunkers, and supply dumps. The devastation they cause means that attack aircraft do not have to revisit their targets, and ground forces do not need to engage in extended campaigns of fire and maneuver. Instead, with survivable delivery systems and a carefully selected list of targets, nuclear weapons used tactically can produce in the space of hours many of the same effects that would take conventional forces many days or weeks to duplicate, with the important difference that both sides would probably collapse quickly under the shock of the nuclear effects. In sum, the same questions arise in determining the size and composition of the tactical nuclear capabilities as face the strategic nuclear planners. What should constitute the target list for the single integrated tactical operational plan (perhaps to be labeled SITOP), and what damage expectancy should be sought against each of the targets?

Target lists are not difficult to find. Table 4-2 shows one set drawn from the central region of Europe. Besides what might be considered standard air superiority and interdiction aiming points, it contains a number of troop targets. They are assumed to represent battalions of ground forces aligned on the forward edge of the battle area (FEBA). Because of their nature they can be treated as discrete aiming points and attacked individually with low-yield weapons delivered by artillery, as the Army would prefer to do. Alternatively, they can be considered as area targets and attacked with higher-yield airburst warheads delivered by longer-range cruise missiles, rockets, or ballistic missiles. If U.S. Army practice were followed, as many as 1,088 weapons would have to be delivered to destroy the first echelon of enemy troops. If higher-yield weapons of about ten kilotons were used, and the entire front were

Table 4-2. **Hypothetical Target List under the Single Integrated Tactical Operational Plan**

	Distance east of inter-German frontier (kilometers)				
Type of target	0–30	30–100	100–300	300–800	Total
Fixed					
Airfields (main operating bases)	. . .	13	31	28	72
Choke points (bridges, railyards, highways, obstructions)	12	10	91	78	191
Bunkers (command, fuel, nuclear storage)	5	27	87	43	162
Subtotal	17	50	209	149	425
Mobile					
Maneuver and artillery battalions[a]	832	132	426	294	1,684
Nuclear missiles and support units	256	129	104	87	576
Subtotal	1,088	261	530	381	2,220
Total	1,105	320	739	530	2,685

Source: Erhard Heckmann, "Requirements and Weaponry," *Military Technology*, vol. 7 (May 1983), pp. 38–60.

a. Many of these individual targets can be grouped into a smaller number of area targets and subjected to barrage attacks.

barraged with them, only 390 delivered weapons would be needed to produce the same devastating effects. In both instances, if more control were wanted, options could be developed to withhold some or all of these attacks.

If the choice appears to offer a distinction without a difference in an era of nuclear plenty, except that the Army preference sounds more discriminating and humane, it is worth recalling several features of current nuclear deployments. Artillery pieces, because they must operate close to the FEBA, are vulnerable to such barrage tactics, for which Soviet delivery systems are eminently suited. Airfields, on which a large number of the longer-range, dual-purpose allied delivery systems are located, are also vulnerable and could easily be destroyed by Soviet ballistic missiles. Accordingly, three conditions have to be met if the United States and its allies are to have more than the facade of a useful tactical nuclear capability. First, dependence on artillery and tactical aircraft will have to be minimized or eliminated, especially since those systems are more valuable in their nonnuclear role and should not be tied down with nuclear missions or training. Second, planners should turn to mobile missiles that can operate at a considerable distance from the front, attributes that would make them more difficult to acquire as targets and less susceptible to barrage attacks. Third, the resulting capability should be single purpose in function, dedicated to second-strike nuclear retaliation, and separated from the conventional forces—

with its own command, control, and communications, and with its own alerting procedures.

Current Effectiveness

That, obviously, is not the kind of capability the United States and its allies deploy today. As a consequence, to use the central region of Europe as an example, the effectiveness of the capability depends heavily on its being used in a first strike, especially if the Pershing IIs and GLCMs are not available for tactical strikes (and perhaps even if they are, depending on how they would be deployed and operated in a crisis). However, if the Soviet Union were to preempt and embark on a first strike of its own (as hypothesized in table 4-3), using barrage tactics against the allied front, NATO could expect, at best, to achieve a damage expectancy of only 27 percent against the targets listed in table 4-2. Moreover, the NATO countries could expect to suffer about 9 million prompt fatalities and another 3 million casualties, even assuming that the Soviet Union airburst all its weapons and attempted to limit the collateral damage to civilians from its attack. Very little would stand in the way of a subsequent occupation of Western Europe by Soviet forces.

These results conceal several grim ironies. The first is that the United States has deployed far more nuclear weapons to Europe than are needed to cover a comprehensive target list but has not provided the survivable delivery systems to go with them. Thus after a Soviet first strike, Europe is rich in warheads and poverty stricken in launchers. The second is that, after all the economic and political costs associated with the deployment of the Pershing IIs and GLCMs, they apparently have no role in the one contingency in which they might prove useful. The third and parallel irony is that neither the warheads in the British and French SSBNs nor the Poseidon warheads committed by the United States to the supreme allied commander, Europe (SACEUR) would presumably be available— or available in a timely enough fashion—to attack critical targets in Eastern Europe. As a result, short of a wholesale retargeting of Pershing IIs, GLCMs, and SSBNs, a serious gap exists in NATO's second-strike coverage of a reasonably prudent but not very demanding target list.

The Role of the Navy

In principle, the Navy already has or is developing enough nuclear delivery systems to fill this gap. Its carriers are likely to have both nuclear-capable aircraft and nuclear weapons on board; its resurrected battleships are equipped to launch nuclear-capable Tomahawk cruise missiles; even its nuclear-powered attack submarines (SSNs) are being armed with the TLAM-N (Tomahawk land-attack missile, nuclear), and surface combatants will be able to launch these cruise missiles as well. Indeed, Navy plans call for the production of perhaps as many as 900 TLAM-Ns. At hand, therefore, are nuclear delivery systems with the survivability, endurance, accuracy, and control that is as necessary to tactical as to strategic nuclear deterrence.

Unfortunately, there are several practical problems with using carriers, surface combatants, and attack submarines as platforms for nuclear launchers. The Navy has never been averse to giving its platforms a dual-purpose capability. But it properly sees the main function of these platforms as being the deterrence and conduct of conventional war. Therefore, it has resisted having its most treasured assets tied down to the peculiar demands of nuclear war plans, with their emphasis on high alert rates, specific launch locations or areas, and preselected targets (for aircraft as well as missiles).

This is not an unreasonable attitude, particularly as regards the attack submarines, which would have key roles and missions to play in a conventional war at sea. But it could also mean that the submarines would be out of position or not programmed for appropriate targets if a conventional war turned nuclear. Furthermore, an element of mystery hovers over just what targets the Navy proposes to cover with the TLAM-N, which has an estimated range of more than 1,500 miles. This uncertainty, combined with issues about the availability of the attack submarines (the most survivable of the TLAM-N platforms), thus makes a delivery system of great potential value for tactical nuclear deterrence something of a question mark.

Program Possibilities

This difficulty does not preclude other solutions to the current vulnerability of the tactical nuclear capabilities and the gap in their coverage of targets in Europe on a second strike. The Army is considering a nuclear version of the MLRS (multiple-launch rocket system), which is mobile and has sufficient range to fire from outside the vulnerable area close to the FEBA. It should also be possible to develop an improved and more mobile version of the older Lance missile, although that would

Table 4-3. Effects of a Soviet Nuclear First Strike and a NATO Tactical Nuclear Second Strike[a]

Item	Alert weapons[b]	Ballistic missiles[c]	Cruise missiles[d]	Fighter-attack aircraft bases	Medium bomber bases	Logistic choke points	Command and storage bunkers	Troop targets[d]	Total
Targets in central region of Europe	...	126	116	52	16	200	200	700	1,410
Soviet forces									
900 artillery	720	...	...	...	...	...	...	720	720
576 short-range missiles	461	...	...	...	...	8	...	453	461
648 fighter-attack aircraft	518	...	...	94	...	224	200	...	518
72 SS-12 ballistic missiles	58	...	...	52	...	6	...	...	58
840 medium-range, intermediate-range ballistic missiles	672	126	116	52	16	162	200	...	672
630 medium bombers (3 weapons per bomber)	1,512	504	348	114	146	200	200	...	1,512
All alert weapons	3,941	630	464	312	162	600	600	1,173	3,941
Delivered weapons	...	441	325	218	113	420	420	821	2,758
Targets destroyed	...	63	58	52	16	195	195	681	1,260
Damage expectancy (percent)	...	50	50	100	100	97.5	97.5	97.3	89.4

Targets in Eastern Europe						
NATO forces	...	72	191	162	832	1,257
1,093 artillery	30	...	...	...	30	30
77 Honest John rockets	2	...	...	...	2	2
42 Pluton missiles	1	...	1	...	...	1
97 Lance missiles	49	...	...	49	...	49
1,300 fighter-attack aircraft	1	1	...	...	...	1
97 Pershing I missiles	48	48	...	...	...	48
18 medium-range missiles	...	...	...	...	...	...
16 medium-range bombers	...	...	...	...	...	...
116 cruise-missile launchers	...	...	...	...	...	...
(4 missiles per launcher)	232	...	190	42	...	232
108 Pershing II missiles	54	23	...	31	...	54
Alert weapons	417	72	191	122	32	417
Delivered weapons	...	58	153	98	26	335
Targets destroyed	...	58	153	98	26[e]	335
Damage expectancy (percent)	...	80.6	80.1	60.5	3.1	26.7

Sources: Tables 4-1, 4-2; and author's estimates.

a. Assumes a Soviet surprise attack and NATO forces on generated alert.

b. For NATO forces, alert surviving weapons.

c. It is assumed, perhaps optimistically, that the USSR can target only 50 percent of the Lance, Pershing, and ground-launched cruise missiles.

d. The USSR uses barrage tactics against a NATO front of 750 kilometers; it is able to cover the entire front with 391 low-yield weapons.

e. NATO does not use barrage tactics against the Warsaw Pact front.

Table 4-4. Effects of a NATO Second Strike If Submarine-based Cruise Missiles Are Added to the Tactical Nuclear Forces[a]

Item	Alert surviving weapons	Fighter-attack aircraft bases	Logistic choke points	Command and storage bunkers[b]	Troop targets[b]	Total
Targets in Eastern Europe	...	72	191	162	832	1,257
NATO forces[c]						
97 Lance missiles	49[d]	...	...	—...	49	49
97 Pershing I missiles	48[d]	...	...	...	48	48
116 cruise-missile launchers (4 missiles per launcher)	232[d]	...	...	...	232	232
108 Pershing II missiles	54[d]	...	...	...	54	54
7 Poseidon submarines (672 cruise missiles) TLAM-N	518[e]	72	191	162	93	518
Alert weapons without TLAM-N	383	...	...	...	383	383
Alert weapons with TLAM-N	901	72	191	162	476	901
Targets destroyed without TLAM-N	...	...	...	...	652	652
Targets destroyed with TLAM-N	...	58	153	130	697	1,038
Damage expectancy (percent) without TLAM-N	...	...	...	...	78.4	51.9
Damage expectancy (percent) with TLAM-N	...	80.6	80.5	80.2	83.8	82.6

Sources: Tables 4-1, 4-2, 4-3; and author's estimates.
a. Assumes a Soviet surprise attack and NATO forces on generated alert.
b. It is assumed that NATO uses barrage tactics and that 383 weapons (airburst) can cover a front of 750 kilometers.
c. Artillery, Honest John, and fighter-attack aircraft no longer are given a nuclear role in U.S. plans and programs.
d. It is assumed, as in table 4-3, that only 50 percent of the Lance, Pershing, and ground-launched cruise missiles are targeted in the Soviet attack.
e. Six of the Poseidon submarines are on station with 576 Tomahawk (land-attack, nuclear) cruise missiles; of this total, 90 percent are on alert.

almost certainly be more expensive. Production lines remain open for both the Pershing II and the GLCM. They too would be more survivable than artillery and aircraft. However, these missiles are expensive to acquire and maintain, and it would make little sense to add them to the existing deployments if they could not be assigned tactical targets and might be negotiated out of deployment overseas in an arms control agreement. In any event, in both the tactical and the strategic nuclear realm, submarines have a comparative advantage over land-mobile launchers, especially when the land is as crowded as Western Europe. Quite understandably, Europeans—like Americans—are less than enthusiastic about having alert nuclear delivery systems wandering in their midst during peacetime or in a crisis. It is therefore customary to park land-mobile launchers at bases that are known and easy to attack. Only in a great emergency or at the outset of a conventional conflict would they presumably move out of these bivouacs.

Submarines, by contrast, have the advantage of being both mobile and invisible when they are out of port. And—depending on the range of their missiles and their target assignments—they are able to move about at will over substantial areas, whether in peacetime or during a crisis. Allies cannot pat them or point, however tremulously, to their presence and to the commitment they allegedly entail on the part of the United States. But if propinquity is of any importance, as is so frequently asserted, the full panoply of U.S. military power, including many land-based nuclear weapons, is almost certain to remain in Europe for the foreseeable future. The allies thus will have much to pat, much to reassure them, and much to criticize for many years to come even if a portion of the tactical nuclear deterrent goes out to sea.

The question nonetheless remains: what platforms are to be made available for the mission? Additional attack submarines bought solely to cover tactical targets with nuclear weapons are obviously too expensive an answer at over $800 million a boat. So would be the acquisition of more Trident SSBNs. However, as the United States retires its older Poseidon SSBNs nothing will prevent the Navy from converting some of them to cruise missile platforms.

It may be too much to hope, but suppose that Pershing IIs, GLCMs, and all allied missiles in Europe, excluding the French Pluton, were committed to the SITOP. To fill the current gap in target coverage would require 7 Poseidon SSBNs, each with 12 cruise missile launchers and 96 missiles, and with 80 percent on station in a crisis (see table 4-4).

Such a change would not be free. Although the hull integrity of the boats themselves is reported to be excellent despite their age, their SLBM compartments (removed as they are taken out of service) would have to be replaced with launchers for cruise missiles, and their nuclear reactors would need substantial reworking. Even so, they would provide what the United States should have and has lacked for many years; namely, the core of an assured, second-strike tactical nuclear deterrent.

CHAPTER FIVE

CONVENTIONAL DEMAND
AND NAVAL SUPPLY

DESPITE the threat of nuclear capabilities and the morbid fascination they exercise, they obviously play a limited role in this turbulent and largely traditional world. Strategic and tactical nuclear launchers loom in the background, while conventional forces occupy stage center and remain the principal military actors, whether in the United States or in the Soviet Union.

This situation is hardly surprising. As the Navy itself points out so frequently, in trying to justify the size and composition of its proposed fleet, the United States since World War II has assumed more than forty commitments to countries or groups of nations around the world. Because of its economic strength and military power the United States has become the leader of and chief contributor to the postwar system of collective security. As such, while rejecting vehemently the role of international policeman, it is seen as the principal opponent of aggression, terrorism, or other challenges to the current order and peaceful change.

With such a burden of responsibilities, and with the primary duty of preserving the territorial integrity and freedom of this country and the lives and liberties of its citizens, the government is bound to try to limit the liability of the United States when it becomes militarily involved overseas. The use of nuclear weapons, or even the threat to use them, except as a bluff or in response to a nuclear attack, is therefore not an option that has aroused much enthusiasm among American leaders. Presidents may continue to declare that they will engage in the first use of nuclear weapons should U.S. and allied defenses fail in Europe or elsewhere. But like President Reagan, all of them have believed, if they have not said, that a nuclear war cannot be won and must never be fought.[1]

1. *Department of Defense Annual Report, Fiscal Year 1985*, p. 38.

Table 5-1. Total Obligational Authority for the Nuclear and Conventional Forces, Fiscal Years 1980–86[a]
Amounts in billions of fiscal 1987 dollars

Year	Nuclear forces[b]	General purpose forces[c]	Year	Nuclear forces[b]	General purpose forces[c]
1980			*1984*		
Amount	43.6	156.0	Amount	71.1	213.7
Percent	21.8	78.2	Percent	25.0	75.0
1981			*1985*		
Amount	45.4	176.7	Amount	70.5	228.0
Percent	20.4	79.6	Percent	23.6	76.4
1982			*1986*		
Amount	51.2	198.1	Amount	70.6	235.9
Percent	20.5	79.5	Percent	23.0	77.0
1983					
Amount	58.4	211.9			
Percent	21.6	78.4			

Sources: Office of the Assistant Secretary of Defense (Comptroller), *National Defense Budget Estimates for 1987*, p. 77; and author's estimates.

a. Total obligational authority (TOA) is a financial measurement that may include some prior-year funding made available for current obligation and other financial adjustments. It can be somewhat larger or smaller than budget authority (BA).

b. Consists of program I (strategic forces), the tactical nuclear capabilities in program II (general purpose forces), half of program III (intelligence and communications), and shares of program VI (research and development) and the three major support programs (VII, VIII, and IX).

c. Comprises most of program II (general purpose forces), half of program III (intelligence and communications), all of programs IV (airlift and sealift), V (national guard and reserve), and X (support of other nations), and appropriate shares of programs VI (research and development), VII, VIII, and IX (support programs).

Any reconciliation of this view with the heavy and unavoidable responsibilities of the United States inevitably leads to a major dependence on conventional capabilities. For that reason, despite the dream of a leakproof defense against nuclear weapons—the equivalent of placing the United States inside an extremely sturdy astrodome—nearly 80 percent of the U.S. defense budget goes to the acquisition of nonnuclear forces (see table 5-1).

Shaping the Demand

Force planners have always faced a difficult problem in determining what should be the size and composition of conventional forces. Critics may see the United States as aggressively inclined; Marxists may consider it driven by the last stages of capitalism and imperialism. But if either group were ever to look at the uncomfortable life of the force planner, it might want to reconsider its theories.

In the isolationist years of the 1920s and well into the 1930s, American force planners had trouble identifying an enemy, much less figuring out what sins he might commit. In desperation, they imagined an invasion by Britain and Canada, gallantly defeated at Saratoga. And once more they struck back at Mexico and defeated its forces on the heights of Chapultepec, all fortunately (at least for the historian) on paper.[2]

In the aftermath of World War II a plethora of enemies materialized, led by the Soviet Union. Still, a number of obstacles to systematic force planning remained. Whatever the rhetoric of the day, the United States and its friends had no stomach for a crusade to liberate Eastern Europe, unhorse the Kremlin, or replace Mao Tse-tung with Chiang Kai-shek. Consequently, there could be no Schlieffen Plan to which the force planners could turn for guidance on the forces needed to execute it. The United States did become wedded to the idea of containment and even practiced it to some degree. But containment gave little help to planners either. It handed the initiative to the potential enemy, which meant that he could choose the time, place, and method of attack. Moreover, since the Soviet Union allegedly possessed overwhelming conventional forces and excellent interior lines of communication, it might decide to attack in several places at once and simultaneously instigate still further aggression by such cohorts as China and North Korea.

One way to have dealt with all these possibilities would have been to build a defensive wall around the periphery of the communist bloc. However, it quickly became evident that, even with substantial contributions from allies, the drain on the United States of large, permanent overseas garrisons would prove unacceptable. By the 1960s it also became evident that the Soviet Union lacked the ability to sustain large offensive operations in two or more separate theaters of war. By the 1970s, with the defection of China from the bloc, if not from communism, a question even arose about the Kremlin's ability to dictate the actions of its remaining cohorts. Force planners nonetheless were left with serious uncertainties. What were the contingencies for which the United States should prepare? How many of them should it expect to occur and deal with simultaneously? What should be the nature of the response?

2. See Dana Mead, "United States Peacetime Strategic Planning, 1920–1941: The Color Plans to the Victory Program" (Ph.D. dissertation, Massachusetts Institute of Technology, 1967). See also Donald Cameron Watt, *Too Serious a Business: European Armed Forces and the Approach to the Second World War* (University of California Press, 1975), p. 96.

How should the United States and its allies share the burden? For how long a war should they prepare?

Force planners, for the most part without any useful guidance from the president, the National Security Council, or the Department of State, have in effect developed several rules to deal with these uncertainties and questions. Since no one knows where, when, how, or even whether the Soviet Union might attack, hypothetical contingencies should be developed as a basis for planning the conventional force inventory. These contingencies should reflect not only known concentrations of military power by the Soviet Union or other potential enemies, but also such areas of vital interest to the United States as Western Europe, Japan, South Korea, the oil-producing states in the Middle East, and the Caribbean.

Specific attacks should be hypothesized so as to reflect enemy strengths and to create severe challenges in the form of surprise and speed in the attacks. But mobilization schedules, troop movements, force readiness and the like should not exceed the limits of physical possibility and plausibility. So far as allies are involved in the hypothetical responses, they should be encouraged to maximize their force contributions. For planning purposes, however, these contributions should be treated as fixed rather than variable, and the United States should make up the difference between the allied input and the alleged need. In determining that need, planners should assume that in the initial stages of the hypothetical war the alliance (if there is one) will conduct a forward defense of the threatened territory. Forward defense is preferable to trading space for time not only because it is more efficient to hold forward than to retreat and later recover the lost territory, but also because it is more expedient to prepare for such a defense than to inform an ally in advance that its territory will have to be sacrificed to strengthen the defense.

How long a campaign the planners should prepare for, and what stocks of war reserve equipment and supplies they should accumulate, inevitably cause disputes, especially considering the high cost of these stocks (currently estimated at more than $115 billion). At one end of the spectrum is the traditional school, which argues that the reserve stocks should be sufficient to tide the fighting forces over until their needs can be met from current U.S. production, a period often estimated, on the average, at six months. At the other end is what might be labeled the short-war school, which usually anticipates that after no more than thirty days of intense combat the war will have either ended or escalated to a nuclear exchange. A more prevalent attitude, dictated in part by the high cost of modern munitions, is that U.S. and allied forces should hold at least enough war reserve stocks to outlast the enemy, a time frequently estimated as lasting between forty-five and sixty days.

Exactly how many of these contingencies might arise more or less simultaneously, and for how many of them the United States should prepare a more or less simultaneous response, depend on several factors. The first is the ability and willingness of the Soviet Union to operate in more than one theater and the likelihood that states such as North Korea, Vietnam, and Cuba might choose to exploit the situation for their own ends. The second is the conservatism with which the planning is to be done, since the larger the number of simultaneous contingencies and responses there are, the greater will be the size of the U.S. forces needed to deal with them.

In the 1960s, when the Soviet Union and China were still thought to be in partnership and Cuba had become a perennial thorn in the side of the United States, two major contingencies, one in Europe and one in Asia, and a minor one in the Caribbean, constituted the basis for planning U.S. conventional forces. As American participation in the war in Vietnam declined and the split between the Soviet Union and China became evident, President Richard M. Nixon essentially dropped the major Asian contingency. Presidents Gerald R. Ford and James E. Carter endorsed this change and continued to base conventional force planning on one major and one minor contingency (with increasing emphasis on the Persian Gulf as a source of the minor contingency). By the late 1970s, however, the goals for U.S. ground forces and land-based tactical air forces had come to resemble strongly the objectives set in the 1960s, at least as far as the active-duty forces were concerned.

The Reagan administration established still more ambitious goals for the conventional forces, even though it was and remains much less clear than its predecessors about the basis for its force goals. However, the ambiguity may reflect more the relative emptiness of official public statements on defense than it does any change in the methodology of the planners. Indeed, all the signs indicate that threats to Europe, the Persian Gulf, Korea, and the Caribbean still provide the main contingencies from which the nonnuclear force structure is derived.

However many of these contingencies the force planners explore, they usually have three expectations about the capabilities recommended

**Table 5-2. U.S. Military Personnel in Foreign Areas, End of Fiscal Years
1976, 1980, 1985**
Thousands

Area	1976	1980	1985
NATO			
Germany	213	244	247
Other Europe	61	65	75
Europe, afloat	41	22	36
Total	315	331	358
Northeast Asia			
South Korea	39	39	42
Japan (including Okinawa)	45	46	47
Total	84	85	89
Other			
Pacific area	27	15	16
Pacific, afloat	24	15	20
Miscellaneous	8	42	32
Total	59	72	68

Source: *Department of Defense Annual Report, Fiscal Year 1987*, table 4, app. B, p. 320.

for deployment. The first is that the forces will, at a minimum, provide a reasonable deterrent to attack in areas of critical interest to the United States. The second is that, since overseas deployments—primarily in NATO and Northern Asia (see table 5-2)—will be minimized, a large force (with intercontinental mobility in the form of airlift and sealift) will exist at most times in the United States, ready to move out and deal with such other crises and attacks as the president and Congress might direct. The third is that decisions about the longer-term conduct and termination of a conventional war involving the United States cannot be made at the outset of such a conflict. Only after the conclusion of the initial and mostly defensive phase can the forces be mobilized and the objectives set for bringing an acceptable end to the war. Consequently, although more comprehensive plans may exist (witness the so-called maritime strategy), the deployed forces are not intended to do more than ensure a satisfactory outcome to the initial and largely defensive phase of the conflict.

Obviously, the forces derived on this basis could not be expected to deal with every conceivable situation. However, if conservative calculations are made, these forces should be sufficient to deal with the cases most threatening to the interests of the United States. Under less demanding conditions they should have more than enough power and mobility to cope with unanticipated emergencies, whether in Grenada or Libya, or on a larger scale.

What the Navy Can Supply

Although there is a recurrent controversy about whether the United States and its allies should plan to fight primarily on land or follow some kind of a maritime strategy as a substitute, the controversy is largely sterile. As far as Europe, the area of the Persian Gulf, and Korea are concerned, the United States is heavily committed to defend its allies with its ground and tactical air forces at or near their frontiers. Otherwise it would not be making such a large investment in land-based capabilities or deploying nearly six large divisions in West Germany and another in South Korea. Thus the real issue is the balance between land-based and sea-based forces.

Current foreign deployments and the firm intention to reinforce them heavily in the event of a major emergency mean, at a minimum, that the United States must have the capability to transport troops, equipment, and supplies to distant overseas theaters. Despite the emphasis on acquiring a large number of long-range, wide-bodied airlift aircraft, sealift is usually the most efficient way to reinforce U.S. expeditionary forces and always the most efficient way to resupply them. Consequently, the United States must, at a minimum, invest in sea-control forces and adopt a "maritime strategy" for the use of those forces to protect its sea lines of communication. At a maximum, it can substitute sea-based ground and tactical air forces for their land-bound counterparts.

The range of capabilities the Navy can supply for these functions is impressive. It offers high-performance aircraft on mobile bases, known as aircraft carriers, as well as slower, long-range maritime patrol aircraft based on land. It can deploy ground forces and aircraft on other mobile bases called amphibious ships, some of which even look somewhat like aircraft carriers. In addition, it supplies surface combatants (now including restored World War II battleships), nuclear-powered attack submarines, mines, minesweepers, underway replenishment ships, and a host of support and auxiliary vessels. Some of these capabilities are useful primarily in protecting the sea-lanes. Others are multipurpose and can attack targets at sea or ashore with missiles, gunfire, aircraft, and ground forces.

When looked at as carriers, amphibious ships of various kinds, cruisers, destroyers, frigates, submarines, and other types and classes of ships, the list grows long and confusing, especially since the Navy

Table 5-3. General Purpose U.S. Naval Force Packages

Type of ship	Carrier battle group	Marine amphibious brigade	100-ship convoy	Submarine barrier	Submarine forward patrol force
			Number of ships		
Aircraft carriers (conventional or nuclear-powered)	1	. . .	. . .	. . .	. . .
Amphibious ships (various types)	. . .	18	. . .	. . .	. . .
Attack submarines (nuclear-powered)	2	. . .	. . .	30	6
Guided-missile cruisers (with Aegis anti-air system)	1	. . .	. . .	. . .	. . .
Destroyers/guided-missile destroyers	5	4	1	. . .	. . .
Mine countermeasures ships	. . .	10	. . .	. . .	. . .
Underway replenishment ships (various types)	4	. . .	. . .	. . .	. . .
Frigates/guided-missile frigates	4	3	9	. . .	. . .
Auxiliaries (various types)	2	4	1	3	1
Total	19	39	11	33	7

Sources: Peter T. Tarpgaard and Robert E. Mechanic, *Future Budget Requirements for the 600-Ship Navy* (Congressional Budget Office, 1985), p. 5; and author's estimates.

uses an arcane and changing set of designators for its units.[3] Fortunately, however, it is possible to aggregate many of the ships into packages related in part to the functions they perform, which is the way they are often considered for purposes of force planning (see table 5-3). Thus there are the various ships, submarines, and aircraft that make up a carrier battle group (CVBG), the amphibious ships and their escorts necessary to transport and land a Marine amphibious brigade (MAB), the number of attack submarines needed to establish a defense barrier in relatively narrow waters, the surface combatants to escort and provide a close-in defense of a large convoy of transports, the fixed and towed sonar systems that provide the underwater early warning and tracking systems against enemy submarines, the patrol aircraft to search for and attack enemy submarines (and now surface combatants) in a large ocean area, and the auxiliary ships needed to support and maintain these packages and perform many miscellaneous functions.

The size of the U.S. fleet should depend on how many of these packages the force planners deem necessary. And the number of packages should depend, as for the land-based forces, on the nature and size

3. For a list of ship designators used by the Department of the Navy, see appendix A. Designators by major ship function are in appendix B, and other key abbreviations used by the Department of the Navy are in appendix C.

of the threats, the contributions that allied navies could make, the types and number of simultaneous contingencies the fleet should be expected to handle, the specific missions U.S. naval forces would perform, and the objectives they would be expected to achieve. It is this kind of assessment and accounting that the Army and the Air Force regularly provide and that is so lacking in the *The Maritime Strategy*. Since the leaders of the Navy do not provide it, an effort must be made to do so in their stead.

CHAPTER SIX

ENEMIES AND ALLIES

IT IS possible to exaggerate the importance of numbers when comparing military capabilities. The relative power and survivability of individual units also count, as the machine gun demonstrated against the rifle. Still, whether the individual units of account are militarily equivalent (a rare event) or not, the number of units on each side remains of interest. Consequently, accurate addition and subtraction are an indispensable tool when it comes to force planning.

The Soviet Navy

The current estimate of the Soviet Navy provided in *Soviet Military Power,* an official publication of the Department of Defense, stands at 1,338 ships and 1,645 aircraft. Secretary of the Navy Lehman, not surprisingly, raises the ante still further and cites the "1,700 ships and submarines that the Soviets can deploy against us."[1] Whether one believes either or neither estimate, the difference in the numbers suggests that adding up naval vessels is less than an exact science. That, however, is not quite the case. The counting problem does not come from any great difficulty in identifying Soviet ships, despite efforts by the Soviet Union to hide or camouflage some of them and create dummies of others.

The problem instead is one of definition. For example, the chief of naval operations claimed as late as 1985 that the Soviet Union deployed 1,423 surface combatants. But he did not add that probably no more than 286 of them were oceangoing ships. He also counted up 380 submarines

1. Admiral James D. Watkins, U.S. Navy, *The Maritime Strategy* (Annapolis: U.S. Naval Institute, 1986), p. 33.

but neglected to break this number down to show that 79 were SLBM platforms and that, of the remaining 301, as many as 173 were diesel-electric powered.[2]

Perhaps more important, when only oceangoing ships and long-range attack submarines are counted, and they are distributed among the four main Soviet fleets, the numbers look less formidable still (see table 6-1). Of the four fleets, the two in the Black Sea and the Baltic would have to travel through very narrow waters controlled by U.S. allies in order to reach the principal sea-lanes between America and Europe. Even without the presence of U.S. naval forces, they would face significant allied capabilities that could keep them out of the Atlantic and control major portions of the Baltic and the Mediterranean. It is therefore the Soviet Northern Fleet, based along the Kola Peninsula near Murmansk, and the Pacific Fleet at Vladivostok and Petropavlovsk that constitute the primary threats from the standpoint of the U.S. Navy.

These two fleets, between them, contain the SSBNs that are a key component of the Soviet strategic nuclear deterrent. They also deploy 156 surface combatants and at least 231 attack submarines (including 90 with diesel-electric power). Together, they constitute a potential threat of serious proportions, even without the exaggerations of such publicists as the Defense Intelligence Agency.

Exactly how the Soviet Union might use its naval forces in a conflict has been the subject of considerable debate and investigation. Current Soviet doctrine suggests that the main function of its general purpose naval forces would be to establish and protect sanctuaries for its SSBNs in waters such as the North Norwegian and Barents seas and the Arctic Ocean in the west and comparable areas in the Far East. Indeed, much of *The Maritime Strategy*, with its emphasis on forward operations and putting Soviet SSBNs at risk, seems designed to force the Soviets to do just that. It is also conceivable, however, that some portion of the naval aviation, surface combatants, and attack submarines of the Northern and Pacific fleets would be committed to attacks on the U.S. sea lines of communication to Norway, Central Europe, the Persian Gulf, and Northeast Asia. Moreover, the Soviet navy has a long history of seeking ways to destroy U.S. SSBNs and aircraft carriers, which seems no less provocative than what *The Maritime Strategy* proposes to do, at least

2. See *The 600-Ship Navy and the Maritime Strategy,* Hearings before the Seapower and Strategic and Critical Materials Subcommittee of the House Armed Services Committee, 99 Cong. 1 sess. (GPO, 1986).

Table 6-1. The Soviet Navy Distributed by Area

Type of force	Northern Fleet (Murmansk)	Baltic Fleet (Leningrad)	Black Sea Fleet (Odessa)	Caspian Sea flotilla	Pacific Fleet (Vladivostok)	Total	Northern and Pacific Fleets only
Ballistic missile submarines	39	6	...	...	25	70	64
Aircraft carriers	1	...	...	...	2	3	3
Principal surface combatants	73	45	74	5	83	280	156
Attack submarines	141	39	35	...	90	305	231
Naval aviation	425	260	450	...	510	1,645	935
Naval infantry brigades	1	1	1	...	2	5	3
Other combat ships	78	95	71	28	120	392	198
Auxiliaries	95	45	51	7	90	288	185

Source: Department of Defense, *Soviet Military Power, 1986* (Government Printing Office, 1986). pp. 12–14.

on paper. Consequently, the U.S. Navy needs to hedge against both eventualities.

If the Soviet navy should venture forth on such missions, it would labor under a number of natural and self-imposed handicaps. As matters now stand, whether coming from the area of Murmansk or Vladivostok, Soviet aircraft, surface combatants, and attack submarines would have to pass over or through narrow waters controlled by U.S. allies to reach vital shipping lanes. From Murmansk, for example, a Soviet attack submarine would have to run between the North Cape of Norway and Spitzbergen, speed down the Norwegian Sea, and transit one of the straits that separate Greenland, Iceland, and Great Britain before it could enter the main North Atlantic trade routes, a voyage of perhaps 2,000 miles. A sortie from Vladivostok would not have to cover as great a distance to get on station. But it would have to run through one of the four narrow straits that lead from the Sea of Japan into the Pacific, perhaps an even more hazardous journey. To make matters worse, because the Soviet navy currently lacks sea-based tactical airpower of any significant range or overseas bases from which to operate long-range fighters, its bombers and surface combatants, after traveling a few hundred miles from their home ports, would find themselves without air cover, a deficiency for which they cannot adequately compensate with bomber guns or ship-based surface-to-air missiles.

Besides these drawbacks, Soviet capabilities suffer from several other handicaps. In the past, Soviet attack submarines were notoriously fast and noisy. Newer models have grown quieter, but whether the decline in noise has been greater than the rise in sonar performance and the introduction by the U.S. Navy of towed arrays of sonars is uncertain. Moreover, because Soviet ships are, on the average, smaller than their U.S. counterparts—the entire Soviet navy weighs considerably less than the U.S. fleet—they carry smaller loads of ordnance, are less habitable, and are generally less suitable for long cruises. Finally, whatever the exact reason, they spend a good deal more time in port, or at anchor when they operate in such areas as the Mediterranean and the Indian Ocean. It is customary, in this connection, to emphasize that the Soviet navy, once designed almost exclusively for coastal defense, has now become an open-ocean force with the capability for worldwide operations, all of which may be true. But Soviet naval exercises take place most frequently in or near such home waters as the Black and Baltic seas, the Arctic Ocean, and the Seas of Japan and Okhotsk (see table 6-2).

Table 6-2. Frequency of Soviet Naval Exercises by Area

Location	Frequent	Less frequent	Occasional
Barents Sea	x		
Arctic Ocean	x		
Norwegian Sea		x	
Northern North Atlantic		x	
Baltic Sea	x		
North Sea			x
Black Sea	x		
Eastern Mediterranean		x	
Western Mediterranean			x
Caribbean			x
South Atlantic			x
Indian Ocean			x
South China Sea			x
Sea of Japan	x		
Sea of Okhotsk	x		
Northern Pacific-Bering Sea	x		
Mid-Pacific			x

Source: Admiral James D. Watkins, U.S. Navy, *The Maritime Strategy* (Annapolis: U.S. Naval Institute, 1986), fig. 2, p. 7.

During the 1960s, in one of its frequent attempts at justifying an expansive future, the Navy visualized a conflict confined to the seas—perhaps on the model of the War of Jenkins' Ear in 1739 (which soon spread to land)—in which the Soviet and U.S. fleets would battle for naval supremacy, the United States would sweep up all Soviet commercial shipping, and the Soviet Union would lose all its transoceanic trade. Since it turned out that the United States would suffer more economic damage than the Soviet Union in the process, this particular contingency fell out of fashion for force planning purposes. That the maritime strategy can take its place seems altogether implausible. Just as Great Britain discovered in the Napoleonic Wars that it could not defeat a great continental power with naval forces alone (and rediscovered that painful truth in World Wars I and II), so the United States has recognized that pressure on its main enemies must come from large land-based forces, whether in limited or more general conventional conflicts.

In these circumstances the key contingencies that should determine U.S. naval force planning for nonnuclear war are bound to arise out of the need to support land-based operations and prevent the Soviet navy from interfering with or otherwise degrading those operations. Since for force planning purposes, it is usually assumed that land campaigns could be fought simultaneously in Europe, the Persian Gulf area, and Korea, the responsibilities of the Navy would indeed be worldwide and weighty. Moreover, even if only one of these major contingencies were to arise, naval forces—like their land-based counterparts—would undoubtedly have an important role to play in other theaters as well— at a minimum, in trying to deter any spread of the conflict to the disadvantage of the United States.

Allied Contributions

Although the Navy tends to consider itself as the sole adversary of the Soviet navy, it has the good fortune to belong to alliances many of whose members maintain navies of their own. The United States tried to discourage the continuation of these forces during the early 1960s, arguing that they were inefficient considering that each of the lesser naval powers had to incur high overhead costs to deploy a small number of ships. As officials then saw it, the same resources could be more effectively used in building up allied ground and tactical air forces, the capabilities that were seen as being in the shortest supply for contingencies in Europe and Asia.

The case for economies of scale and a more systematic division of labor, however, was no match for British, French, Dutch, and other naval traditions. The consequence is that the NATO countries (excluding the United States) have nearly 400,000 people and more than 600 ocean-going ships in their navies, while the Asian allies of the United States (not counting China) deploy another 120,000 naval personnel and 200 warships (table 6-3). Furthermore, a number of the allies occupy strategic locations along the routes Soviet naval forces would have to follow, and they provide valuable bases from which U.S. ships and aircraft can operate.

Because of these assets, allied naval forces can share the burdens of the Navy in many ways. Allied cruisers, destroyers, and frigates in the Atlantic are sufficient to escort about 17 large convoys a month between the United States and Europe. Similarly, some of the 15 nuclear-powered and 113 diesel-electric submarines in the European navies could contribute significantly to the establishment of barriers against Soviet attack submarines on their way to and from Murmansk. It is even conceivable that the navies of France, Italy, Spain, and Turkey, in conjunction with

Table 6-3. Allied Fleets by Potential Wartime Deployment

Item	Atlantic[a]	Baltic[b]	Mediterranean[c]	Pacific[d]	Total
Personnel	181,090	41,900	176,000	121,025	520,015
Attack carriers	2	...	...	...	2
Antisubmarine warfare carriers	5	...	...	...	5
Cruisers	1	...	2	...	3
Destroyers	40	7	41	72	160
Frigates	125	19	40	44	228
Mine countermeasures ships	57	70	84	62	273
Nuclear-powered attack submarines	15	...	...	...	15
Conventional attack submarines	42	28	43	22	135
Total ships	287	124	210	200	821
Total ships available for convoy duty	171	26	83	116	396

Source: International Institute for Strategic Studies, *The Military Balance, 1985–1986* (London: IISS, 1985).
a. Ocean-going ships from Belgium, Britain, Canada, France, the Netherlands, Norway, and Portugal.
b. Ocean-going ships from Denmark and the Federal Republic of Germany.
c. Ocean-going ships from Greece, Italy, Spain, and Turkey.
d. Ocean-going ships from Australia, Japan, South Korea, and Taiwan.

allied land-based tactical air forces, could substitute for the Sixth Fleet in the Mediterranean, and that Japanese and South Korean submarines could, at a minimum, take responsibility for harassing the Soviet Pacific Fleet in the Seas of Japan and Okhotsk. Japan and South Korea, between them, could also provide considerable support to the U.S. Seventh Fleet in its convoy escort duties.

Perhaps, in a world of more integrated and rationalized armed forces, the United States should concentrate more on naval capabilities and the allies more on ground forces. But the reality is that allied navies exist. They should therefore be considered as assets and taken into account when the United States decides on the size and composition of its own general purpose naval forces.

CHAPTER SEVEN

PROTECTING THE SEA-LANES

EVEN WHEN allied naval forces are taken into account, the U.S. Navy has more than enough to do. First and foremost among its missions is protection of the sea lines of communication to the main potential theaters of war.

The Dimensions of the Problem

Why that mission should have the highest priority in naval force planning is easy to grasp. Whatever the strategic concept adopted by the Reagan administration, a conservative assumption for the future is that the Soviet Union and its cohorts might possibly threaten to undertake three major offensives: in Europe, in Iran, and in Korea. Even supposing that the United States would have stocks of equipment and supplies for forty-five days of combat in or near these theaters, such an emergency would demand prompt preparations for the reinforcement and resupply of its overseas forces.

The total amount of tonnage that would have to be moved overseas is large. By one estimate (shown in table 7-1), it could amount to 4,685 ship transits a month, or more than 500 million tons, assuming that all petroleum products would have to be imported. Of that total, perhaps 7.5 million tons or more a month would probably have to go for the reinforcement and resupply of U.S. forces overseas. If, on the average, each ship assigned to the U.S. effort could transport 10,000 tons, a minimum of 750 ships would be needed each month to move this tonnage, assuming no interference and sinkings by the enemy.

Whether the Soviet Union would actually attack these ships with units from its Northern and Pacific fleets is bound to remain uncertain,

Table 7-1. Illustrative Monthly Ship Transits

Item	Atlantic	Mediter-ranean	Pacific	Indian Ocean	Total
Peacetime					
Economic					
Tankers	2,000	200	550	875	3,625
Dry bulk	5,875	600	4,550	50	11,075
General cargo	8,000	650	4,300	825	13,775
Total	15,875	1,450	9,400	1,750	28,475
Protracted war					
Military					
Tankers	50	10	20	20	100
General cargo	300	100	200	50	650
Subtotal	350	110	220	70	750
Economic					
Tankers	1,200	120	330	525	2,175
Dry bulk	295	30	230	5	560
General cargo	800	65	430	85	1,380
Subtotal	2,295	215	990	615	4,115
Total	2,645	325	1,210	685	4,865

Source: Paul H. Nitze, Leonard Sullivan, Jr., and the Atlantic Council Working Group on Securing the Seas, *Securing the Seas: The Soviet Naval Challenge and Western Alliance Options* (Boulder, Colo.: Westview Press, 1979), p. 163; see also p. 134 for assumptions about ship capacities in metric tons.

especially considering the declared policy of a forward strategy contained in *The Maritime Strategy*. Also uncertain is the number of assets Soviet leaders would commit if they decided to conduct a campaign against allied sea-lanes, and the extent to which they would try to concentrate their forces on U.S. military cargoes. Since, inevitably, assumptions must be made about these issues for purposes of force planning, suppose the following developments in the Atlantic: that with the aid of overhead reconnaissance the Soviet Union could identify and track the U.S. military convoys; that it could vector its attack submarines to intercept them; and that it would commit a total of 67 (or half its long-range operational attack submarines) to this anti-U.S mission alone, at least during the first month of the campaign. If each of these submarines carried 12 torpedoes, and each submarine had an overall kill probability of 25 percent, the force would be able, on the average, to sink 201 U.S. unprotected ships a month, for a total loss during the first month of more than 2 million tons. Under this extreme set of assumptions, the same loss would continue in each succeeding month.

What would be the implications of such a loss? The combination of a U.S. Army division and an Air Force fighter-attack wing might be expected to use roughly 210,000 tons of combat consumables a month.

Consequently, a monthly loss of 2 million tons would effectively put out of action the equivalent of more than 9 U.S. divisions and tactical air wings after little more than a month of combat. If allied forces were otherwise capable of maintaining a forward defense in Central Europe and North Norway, this decline in combat power could make the difference between success and failure in the allied effort.

Solutions to the Problem

One obvious way for the United States to deal with this problem would be to increase still more its stockpiles of war reserve materiel in the key theaters. Such an alternative has several serious drawbacks. First, there is the uncertainty of how large the stocks would have to be, combined with the cost—which could run up to $58 billion worldwide for each additional month of supply. Second, the stockpiles themselves would become increasingly vulnerable to attack from the air, depending on where they were located relative to the fronts and how much active and passive defense they were given. Third, it would do little good for the United States to increase its stocks unless allied forces could be equally well supplied. Finally, war reserves stockpiled in one theater prove extremely difficult to move if an emergency arises in another region. Not only may the transport be in short supply, but host countries may object (as they have in the past) both to the loss of the supplies and to their involvement, however indirect and remote, in a conflict outside their area of responsibility. Thus the United States might find itself in the position of losing the flexibility to react to unanticipated contingencies, which have been the norm rather than the exception in the recent past. Alternatively, it could attempt the even more costly task of stockpiling supplies at every conceivable point of danger, both on land and in maritime pre-positioning ships at sea, as it has done in the Indian Ocean off the island of Diego Garcia. But how to protect the stocks would still remain in question.

Another possibility would be to dispatch enough ships and supplies each month so that, in the Atlantic, for example, even after enemy submarines had sunk more than 2 million tons, enough would get through to meet all the needs of the U.S. expeditionary forces in Europe. This alternative also has several serious drawbacks. Ship crews knowing that they would be almost totally vulnerable to the enemy (even if their transports were armed) might show an understandable reluctance to go to sea. The enemy might be tempted to increase the carnage by risking a larger number of submarines in the first month of the campaign. Furthermore, even without this uncertainty, to acquire the ships and cargoes necessary to compensate for the expected losses would cost about $25 billion for each month of combat. Obviously, a considerable amount of protection could be bought for this amount. Indeed, however unrealistic the option of attempting to saturate or exhaust enemy capabilities with cargo ships, its cost does provide a baseline against which to measure the utility of the various offensive and defensive measures the Navy has at its disposal.

Naval Assets

Basically, the Navy can protect the sea-lanes and their users with two types of defenses. Essentially, they consist of area and point defenses. The area defenses take advantage of the geographic features that favor the United States and its allies in both the Atlantic and the Pacific. As one example, the United States can establish barriers between Greenland and Iceland, and between Iceland and the United Kingdom, by mining the intervening waters and by patrolling them with submarines and aircraft. By the same means, the Navy can blockade the exits into the Pacific from the Sea of Japan. With these barriers in place, and submarines on forward patrol, it becomes possible to intercept and attack any ships or submarines that attempt to run through the passages. This geography also permits the stationing of land-based aircraft in such a way that they can detect and intercept enemy bombers attempting to attack allied naval forces and shipping.

Point defenses, primarily in the form of surface combatants, can surround vital targets and attack enemy units that get through the barrier defenses. The practice of organizing merchant ships into convoys and protecting them with warships has existed for centuries. Its importance has increased with the advent of long-range attack submarines and bombers. Under present conditions, destroyers and frigates armed with antiair and antisubmarine capabilities can provide one ring of defenses around convoys. Helicopters armed with antisubmarine warfare detection and attack equipment, and based on the destroyers and frigates, can form a second ring of defenses at a greater distance from the convoys.

Because the range of ASW detection and attack capabilities has increased, the same number of escorts can protect a larger number of ships than was deemed practicable in World War II. Whereas about 65 ships per convoy was the average then, 100 ships per convoy now appears to be an acceptable number. Moreover, since the current generation of cargo ships is larger and faster, more tonnage can be moved more rapidly than in the past, and turnaround times in port are expected to be shorter.

Counterbalancing these improvements are the additions to the offense of nuclear-powered attack submarines and cruise missiles launched by submarines and aircraft from distances greater than torpedoes can travel. This battle of measures and countermeasures has led some knowledgeable observers to suggest that despite all the changes, the relation between the offense and the defense has not altered appreciably since World War II.[1]

The Nature of the Campaign

If that is indeed the case, the costs of defending the sea-lanes will remain high. The principal reason for these high costs is the attack submarine. It is difficult to believe that the Soviet Union would commit its surface combatants as commerce raiders. They would fall prey to long-range U.S. bombers equipped with air-to-surface missiles, attack submarines on forward patrol, and the area defenses they would have to penetrate to reach the shipping lanes. If committed, they would probably lead exciting but short lives.

The Navy has classified Soviet bombers armed with air-to-surface missiles as a threat equal to the submarines. But the capabilities of these aircraft—and especially of the 100 or more Backfires assigned to Soviet Naval Aviation—appear to have been overstated. Moreover, all of them would have difficulty in selecting routes and flight profiles that escaped U.S. and allied land-based interceptors at such strategic locations as Norway, Iceland, Scotland, Greenland, Korea, and Japan.

Submarines, by contrast, are difficult to detect, classify, track,

1. See "Quantifying the Sealane Problem," in Paul H. Nitze, Leonard Sullivan, Jr., and the Atlantic Council Working Group on Securing the Seas, *Securing the Seas: The Soviet Naval Challenge and Western Alliance Options* (Boulder, Colo.: Westview Press, 1979), chap. 13.

Table 7-2. Effects of a Soviet Attack on the Atlantic Sea-Lanes[a]

U.S. situation	Ships lost					Millions of tons delivered					
	Month				Total	Month				Total	Surplus or shortage
	1	2	3	4		1	2	3	4		
	5 U.S. convoys per month (100 ships per convoy, 10,000 tons per ship)[b]										
1. No protection	201	201	201	201	804	2.99	2.99	2.99	2.99	11.96	−8.04
2. Escorts only	191	172	156	140	659	3.09	3.28	3.44	3.60	13.41	−6.59
3. Escorts and helicopters	181	148	120	98	547	3.19	3.52	3.80	4.02	14.53	−5.47
4. Escorts, helicopters, and open-ocean search	172	127	93	68	460	3.28	3.73	4.07	4.32	15.40	−4.60
5. Escorts, helicopters, open-ocean search, and GIUK barrier[c]	121	43	16	6	186	3.79	4.57	4.84	4.94	18.14	−1.86
6. Escorts, helicopters, open-ocean search, GIUK barrier, and forward patrol[c]	109	32	9	3	153	3.91	4.68	4.91	4.97	18.47	−1.53
	6 U.S. convoys per month (100 ships per convoy, 10,000 tons per ship)[b]										
6. Escorts, helicopters, open-ocean search, GIUK barrier, and forward patrol[c]	109	32	9	3	153	4.91	5.68	5.91	5.97	22.47	2.47

Sources: Nitze and others, *Securing the Seas*, pp. 337–82; and author's estimates.

a. It is assumed that the USSR commits 67 submarines to the attack, that each submarine carries 12 torpedoes, and that each torpedo has a kill probability of .25.

b. The objective is to deliver 5 million tons a month to U.S. forces in Europe and 20 million tons in four months.

c. GIUK stands for Greenland, Iceland, and the United Kingdom.

localize, and hit. They operate in a much less tractable medium than the atmosphere; they can move slowly and quietly; they can take evasive action and engage in deceptive measures; and because the nuclear-powered models do not have to come near the surface to recharge batteries, they offer fewer opportunities than diesel-electric submarines for detection from the air. These characteristics cause ASW systems to be expensive and yet to have relatively low probabilities of kill against attacking submarines. Submarines therefore remain the principal threat to the sea-lanes, and an ASW campaign in the future, as in the past, is expected to be a campaign of attrition lasting for months. During that period the enemy submarines would undergo attack as they proceeded toward the shipping lanes, as they attempted to sink the protected convoys, and as they returned to their home ports for more ordnance, supplies, repairs, and rest for their crews. Once they reembarked, the process of attrition would begin again, as would the losses of U.S. tonnage.

Efficient Defenses

Many factors will determine how long such a campaign might last and what results it might obtain. Not the least of these is the number of area and point defense barriers interposed between the attacking submarines and their targets in the shipping lanes. Table 7-2 illustrates the results of an ASW campaign in the Atlantic as various types of barriers are added to the defense. The assumptions about the Soviet Union are the same as those used in the attack on unprotected shipping. The Soviet Union cycles its submarines so that it keeps the maximum possible number on station and half of them available to attack U.S. shipping during the length of the campaign. Each of the 67 submarines on the anti-U.S. mission carries 12 torpedoes (or cruise missiles); each delivery system has an overall kill probability of 25 percent. However, although the objective of the United States remains the same—the delivery of 5 million tons a month to Europe—the Navy tries to reach it by more traditional means. Each month it dispatches 5 protected convoys, each consisting of 100 ships. Again, in the interests of simplicity, each ship is assumed to carry 10,000 tons of cargo and have a speed of 20 knots. It is also assumed that barriers patrolled by submarines with access to SOSUS data are the most effective (with a 30 percent probability of kill in narrow waters, and a 10 percent probability in wider straits), whereas those entailing the search of large areas of the open ocean and the point defense of the convoys have lower probabilities of kill (5 percent in each instance).

However these assumptions might be changed, as more barriers are added, the number of enemy submarines sunk over a period of four months increases, as does the amount of tonnage delivered. Thus if cost were of no consequence, the conclusion of the analysis would have to be: the more barriers the better. But it is worth noting that here, as elsewhere, the law of diminishing returns to scale comes into play. That is to say, although the cost of adding a barrier remains more or less fixed, effectiveness—whether measured in submarines sunk, or better still in tonnage delivered—rises at a diminishing rate. Indeed, by the time the sixth barrier is added (keeping in mind that the ability to add the more effective area barriers is limited by geography), the saving in tonnage has become relatively small. Yet the acquisition cost has risen from $20.5 billion for the point protection of five convoys to $57.8 billion for the combination of point and area defenses. The addition of a sixth convoy would increase the cost of the ASW protection by $3.9 billion, and the extra supplies would run to another $7.5 billion.

Despite these costs, the most efficient option, given the objective, would be to maintain three area defense barriers—one anchored on Greenland, Iceland, and the United Kingdom (the GIUK barrier), one based further forward, and a third placed to the south that would rely on open ocean search and available tracking data. Added to them would be six instead of five convoys, each with point defenses consisting of two barriers: the surface combatants counted as one, the helicopters as a second. As table 7-2 indicates, this option enables the United States to come close to its goal of 5 million tons a month during the first month of the campaign and to exceed it thereafter. By the end of the fourth month, moreover, the Soviet submarine threat has fallen to minor proportions. Costs, it should be added, are kept well below those incurred in attempting to saturate enemy submarines with unprotected shipping.

ASW defenses in the Pacific and Indian Ocean are similar to those in the Atlantic, even though the geography and the demands are somewhat different. The Soviet Union might attempt to direct as many as 43 of its attack submarines against U.S. convoys during the first month of the campaign. The United States, for its part, would probably want to deliver 650,000 tons a month to Korea and another 1.9 million tons a month to the Persian Gulf in support of what used to be called the rapid deployment force. As in the Atlantic, the Navy could establish barriers in the straits leading out of the Sea of Japan; it could engage in submarine patrols off Petropavlovsk; it has the bases from which to engage in open-area search, principally with patrol aircraft, in both the Western Pacific and the Indian Ocean; and it could plan on at least three protected 100-ship convoys a month to hedge against losses to Soviet attack submarines and still meet the needs of the overseas U.S. forces. A system of five barriers—three consisting of area defenses and two of point defenses around each convoy—could do about as well in this area as in the Atlantic (see table 7-3).

The results, whether for Europe or for Asia, are highly sensitive to the assumptions, which could be made more or somewhat less favorable to the United States. However, the assumptions used to plan the forces (which favor the enemy) and the outcomes are in accord with the general statements about an ASW campaign found in various annual Defense Reports of the secretary of defense, and they coincide reasonably well with the results shown in *Securing the Seas*.[2]

ASW Capabilities

These analyses make it possible to estimate the size, composition, and costs of the forces that the Navy can efficiently devote to the protection of the sea-lanes. Table 7-4 lists the major components of these forces and shows their annual investment and operating costs in 1987 dollars. Most prominently, the ASW system contains 72 nuclear-powered attack submarines, 243 P-3C patrol aircraft, 9 destroyers of the DD-963 class, and 81 FFG-7 frigates. In all, the system consists of 188 ships and submarines. Its annual cost is $19 billion.

Several features about this part of the fleet are worth underlining. First, although ASW is extremely costly, if efficiently designed it remains cheaper than any other way of supporting large U.S. expeditionary forces in wartime. Second, one reason why ASW is so expensive is that its sensors and delivery systems operate from high-priced platforms, whether they be aircraft, destroyers, frigates, or submarines. Some minimum number of these platforms is needed to establish efficient

2. Ibid., pp. 346, 353–57; and *Department of Defense Annual Report, Fiscal Year 1976*, p. III-25, *Fiscal Year 1979*, p. 92, and *Fiscal Year 1981*, p. 114.

Table 7-3. Effects of a Soviet Attack on the Pacific Sea-Lanes[a]

U.S. situation	Ships lost					Millions of tons delivered					Surplus or shortage
	Month				Total	Month				Total[b]	
	1	2	3	4		1	2	3	4		
	3 U.S. convoys per month (100 ships per convoy, 10,000 tons per ship)[b]										
1. No protection	129	129	129	129	516	1.71	1.71	1.71	1.71	6.84	−3.16
2. Escorts only	123	111	100	90	424	1.77	1.89	2.00	2.10	7.76	−2.24
3. Escorts and helicopters	116	95	77	63	351	1.84	2.05	2.23	2.37	8.49	−1.51
4. Escorts, helicopters, and open-ocean search	111	81	60	44	296	1.89	2.19	2.40	2.56	9.04	−0.96
5. Escorts, helicopters, open-ocean search, and Japanese barrier[c]	77	28	10	4	119	2.23	2.72	2.90	2.96	10.81	0.81
6. Escorts, helicopters, open-ocean search, Japanese barrier, and forward patrol[c]	70	20	6	2	98	2.30	2.80	2.94	2.98	11.02	1.02

Sources: Nitze and others, *Securing the Seas*, pp. 337–82; and author's estimates.

a. It is assumed that the USSR commits 43 submarines to the attack, that each submarine carriers 12 torpedoes, and that each torpedo has a kill probability of .25.

b. The objective is to deliver 2.5 million tons a month to U.S. forces in South Korea and the Persian Gulf area and 10 million tons in four months.

c. The Japanese barrier consists of U.S. mines and submarines in key exits from the Sea of Japan and Petropavlovsk. Submarines are on forward patrol in the Seas of Japan and Okhotsk.

Table 7-4. Efficient Force Antisubmarine Warfare Capabilities, Fiscal Year 1997
Billions of fiscal 1987 dollars

System	Annual investment, operating and support cost
SOSUS sound surveillance system with tethered sonars	0.3
26 T-AGOS sound surveillance ships with towed arrays of sonars	0.2
2,500 CAPTOR mines (tethered, encapsulated MK-46 torpedoes with sonar detectors)	0.3
72 SSN-688 nuclear-powered attack submarines	11.0
9 DD-963 antisubmarine warfare destroyers	1.2
81 FFG-7 guided-missile frigates	2.8
180 LAMPS light airborne multipurpose system (a helicopter)	1.0
243 P-3C maritime patrol aircraft, primarily for antisubmarine warfare	2.2
Total (188 ships)	19.0

Sources: Tables 5-3, 7-1, 7-3; and author's estimates.

defenses in several oceans. But the evidence strongly suggests that beyond a certain minimum it becomes more cost effective to improve the performance of sensors and delivery systems than to proliferate platforms and barriers. Indeed, that is only one of many reasons why comparing the size of the U.S. Navy with that of the Soviet navy, or the number of Soviet submarines with those of the United States, is not profitable. Third, as long as the campaign for control of the sea-lanes consists primarily of aircraft and attack submarines attempting to break through a series of barriers to sink cargo, tanker, and transport ships, U.S. amphibious forces have no role in it. Aircraft carriers, on the other hand, have an ASW capability in the form of their very expensive S-3A patrol aircraft, and an antibomber capability with their F-14 and F-18 fighters. However, as long as the United States and its allies retain their current geographic advantages over the Soviet Union, they can operate patrol aircraft and fighters from land bases more efficiently than from the more costly and vulnerable carrier battle groups. Other critical wartime missions—missions that cannot be performed by land-based forces or current ASW capabilities—have to be found to justify the expense of amphibious lift and carrier battle groups.

CHAPTER EIGHT

THE CASE FOR POWER PROJECTION

THE CAMPAIGN over the sea-lanes is usually portrayed as a straightforward duel in which the offense charges into a waiting defense. The offense, however, has several ways of trying to reduce the effectiveness of the area defenses. Perhaps the most obvious of these tactics would be for the Soviet Union to deploy a number of its attack submarines to the key sea-lanes in the Atlantic and Pacific before beginning to attack on land. By itself, this tactic would enable the Soviet submarines to avoid at least three of the five defensive barriers on their first outbound sortie and thereby increase the damage they could do to U.S. convoys during the first month of the war. If, in addition, they could be resupplied at sea, they might be able to make a second attack without having suffered the hazards of the area defenses on their way to and from their home ports.

A second tactic would have the Soviets attempt to reduce the effectiveness of one or more of the area defense barriers by controlling the land on which they would be anchored and actively engaging the barrier forces. To this end, in the past, the U.S. Navy has assumed that the Soviets might seize Iceland by a sudden *coup de main* from the sea, or control both sides of La Perouse Strait between Hokkaido (Japan) and Sakhalin Island, which they already occupy. Perhaps even more promising from the standpoint of the Soviets would be the rapid occupation of North Norway. Not only would that permit them to evade one potential barrier to access to the North Atlantic; it would reduce the distance to the key sea-lanes from 2,000 to 1,000 miles, and thereby enable the Soviets to keep more submarines on station out of the same total force.

A third tactic, probably the most disruptive of all, would be for the Russians to establish the equivalent of home ports for submarines and long-range aircraft outside the natural obstacles that now ring their major naval bases. Such a move, in which the Soviet Union has understandably shown a keen interest, would either reduce the effectiveness of the U.S. antisubmarine warfare system or increase substantially the cost of maintaining the system at the current level of effectiveness. Table 8-1 summarizes the effect of each of these tactics on the ability of the United States to deliver the requisite tonnages to its fighting forces overseas.

It is clearly in the interest of the United States to prevent or reverse any degradation in its ASW defenses. And it surely makes sense to take out reasonable hedges against any such eventuality. But which of these tactics or contingencies should be the Navy's responsibility, which should it be prepared for, and what specific capabilities should it have available for these purposes?

Predeployment

Whether the size and composition of the fleet should be adjusted in any significant way to cope with the contingency of predeployment is open to debate. The Soviets do not now make a habit of deploying large numbers of submarines beyond the key natural barriers in the Atlantic and Pacific. Consequently, a sudden surge of such activity, combined with the mobilization and deployment of ground and tactical air forces in a sensitive theater such as Europe, would be detected and would provide warning of the most serious kind of a major attack. And although this deployment might not give the Navy enough time to set up its main barriers or warrant attacks on Soviet submarines in transit, it would allow other measures to be taken to minimize the effect of a Soviet attack, especially in Europe. In other words, predeployment would not be without serious risks for the Kremlin and does not rate very high in plausibility.

The Navy, in any event, already has in hand certain hedges against this eventuality. The combination of aircraft carriers and amphibious ships already in the fleet takes up more than 50 percent of the surface combatants and 25 percent of the attack submarines for their protection. If the carriers and the amphibious ships could be withheld from early operations, as might prove desirable in a number of circumstances, as many as 112 escorts and 24 attack submarines could be pressed into service for open-ocean search and increased convoy protection. Air

Table 8-1. Effects of Soviet Attempts to Circumvent the U.S. Antisubmarine Warfare System in the Atlantic[a]

| | Ships lost | | | | | Millions of tons delivered | | | | | |
| | Month | | | | | Month | | | | | Surplus or shortage |
Case	1	2	3	4	Total	1	2	3	4	Total	
1. Predeployment (30 submarines)[b]											
5 convoys	141	41	12	4	198	3.59	4.59	4.88	4.96	18.02	-1.98
6 convoys	141	41	12	4	198	4.59	5.59	5.88	5.96	22.02	2.02
2. Predeployment (30 submarines) and one-time resupply (67 submarines)[c]											
5 convoys	141	115	33	10	299	3.59	3.85	4.67	4.90	17.01	-2.99
6 convoys	141	115	33	10	299	4.59	4.85	5.67	5.90	21.01	1.01
3. North Norway seized (67 submarines)[d]											
5 convoys	158	57	21	7	243	3.42	4.43	4.79	4.93	17.57	-2.43
6 convoys	158	57	21	7	243	4.42	5.43	5.79	5.93	21.57	1.57
4. Iceland seized (67 submarines)[e]											
5 convoys	140	67	32	16	255	3.60	4.33	4.68	4.84	17.45	-2.55
6 convoys	140	67	32	16	255	4.60	5.33	5.68	5.84	21.45	1.45
5. Soviet overseas home port (67 submarines)[f]											
5 convoys	181	148	120	98	547	3.19	3.52	3.80	4.02	14.53	-5.47
6 convoys	181	148	120	98	547	4.19	4.52	4.80	5.02	18.53	-1.47

Sources: Paul H. Nitze, Leonard Sullivan, Jr., and the Atlantic Council Working Group on Securing the Seas, Securing the Seas: The Soviet Naval Challenge and Western Alliance Options (Boulder, Colo.: Westview Press, 1979), pp. 337–82; and author's estimates.

a. The U.S. ASW system consists of escorts, helicopters, open-ocean search, the GIUK (Greenland–Iceland–United Kingdom) barrier, and forward patrol.
b. A total of 67 submarines, each with 12 torpedoes, and each torpedo with a kill probability of .25 is committed; 30 of the 67 are predeployed to the main shipping lanes.
c. 67 submarines are committed; 30 are predeployed; all 67 are resupplied on a one-time basis without having to return to home ports.
d. 67 submarines are committed but transit times are cut in half.
e. 67 submarines are committed but GIUK barrier is degraded.
f. 67 submarines operate from an overseas home port in the South Atlantic.

Force B-52s could also substitute for the carriers in searching for and attacking any Soviet ships intended for the resupply of the predeployed Soviet submarines. It is not at all clear, therefore, that predeployment would create any special demand for carriers and amphibious ships or for additional surface combatants and attack submarines.

Barrier Attacks

In the event of a great crisis, Soviet naval leaders might argue in favor of attempting to neutralize the main geographic barriers to their attack submarines. But reasonable readiness and alertness on the part of U.S. and allied navies, particularly their maritime patrol aircraft and submarines—surely to be expected in a crisis—would make a Soviet effort to seize and hold Iceland a risky enterprise. Indeed, its success would depend heavily on surprise, not something easy to achieve when relatively large forces have to be assembled and moved over a considerable distance, whether by air or by sea.

An invasion of South Korea would encounter heavy fortifications as well as South Korean and U.S. ground and tactical air forces. It would be their responsibility (and perhaps that of China) to halt the invasion. In the circumstances carriers and amphibious forces would have no role to play unless South Korean defenses proved far less capable than is generally assumed. And if doubt exists on that score from the standpoint of force planning, the most efficient remedy is more or better land-based forces. Similarly, if the Japanese cannot prevent an invasion of Hokkaido, it is doubtful that U.S. carrier battle groups and amphibious forces could or should do it for them. In any event, the responsibility is one for Japan, and it can be better fulfilled by larger land-based capabilities if the odds do not now favor the Japanese.

Indeed, it is worth stressing again that carrier battle groups and amphibious forces (the main power projection forces), because of their high cost relative to land-based capabilities (as shown in table 8-2), have a role to play only when a contingency arises that is beyond the reach of land-based forces, or when host countries deny the use of land bases. Whatever the plausibility of an adversary's efforts to degrade U.S. ASW capabilities, none of these efforts makes a strong case for buying power projection forces. Of course, to the extent that their acquisition can be supported on other grounds, it will lie with the president and his military

Table 8-2. U.S. Sea-based and Land-based Power Projection Forces Compared
Billions of fiscal 1987 dollars

Component	Acquisition cost
Marine amphibious force	
1 division	2.9
1 wing	5.8
55 amphibious ships (without escorts)	29.0
Total	37.7
Mechanized division[a]	
1 division	6.4
2 close air support and fighter wings (Air Force)	4.3
5 SL-7 fast sealift ships	1.0
5 air refueling tankers	0.5
Total	12.2
Carrier battle group	
1 carrier	2.8
1 wing	5.4
6 escorts	5.7
2 attack submarines	1.8
4 underway replenishment ships	1.5
4 escorts for underway replenishment ships	1.0
Total	18.2
Air Force fighter wing[a]	
1 F-15 wing	6.0
2 airborne warning and control systems	0.6
10 C-5 airlift aircraft	3.0
5 air refueling tankers	0.5
1 F-16 wing (air defense)	2.0
Total	12.1

Source: Author's estimates.
a. Both the mechanized division and the Air Force wing are charged with the cost of moving overseas and establishing air defenses.

advisers to decide how to use them. Thus the issue remains whether other grounds can be found.

North Norway

An attack on north Norway at first glance appears as an ideal justification for amphibious forces and carrier battle groups. Norway is critical to NATO and to the U.S. Navy. The Soviet Union has relatively large forces available for an attack (about 10 divisions and 225 fighter-attack aircraft), whereas Norway has few active-duty units and would probably need allied assistance to prevent the loss of Finnmark (the northernmost part of Norway) at the outset of a war. In recognition of that need, the United States, Great Britain, and Canada have agreed to send early reinforcements in the event of an attack. For better or worse, the United States—with Norwegian agreement—has gone a step further. It has committed itself to the rapid deployment of a Marine Corps brigade and is pre-positioning its equipment in the Trøndelag region in the middle of Norway. But the brigade would presumably not depend on amphibious lift. Instead, it would be flown in to marry up with its equipment and would then move north to join in resisting a Soviet attack, perhaps to be reinforced later by the rest of the division.

Certainly this is a legitimate mission for the Marine Corps, especially since it has more divisions than amphibious lift to move them, and since the standard force planning contingencies make such great demands on other U.S. ground and tactical air forces. But does this decision really lay the groundwork for carrier battle groups and amphibious lift?

As *The Maritime Strategy* makes clear, the Marine Corps sees the Norwegian mission as an opportunity (or an excuse) to engage in amphibious operations, whereas the Navy naturally claims that it will need to cover these operations with carrier-based air. Yet it is evident that neither amphibious lift nor carrier battle groups are essential to the basic mission. Norway certainly wants reinforcements and has provided the facilities on land to receive them. Subsequent land-based operations in defense of north Norway would remain the preferred approach.

Perhaps more will need to be done to deter the Soviet Union from turning this exposed northern flank of NATO. If so, it will be far cheaper for Norway and its allies to make the improvements on land than to invest in amphibious lift and carrier battle groups that would have to fight in the teeth of Soviet power operating from land bases on the Kola Peninsula. Therefore, if the Marine Corps is to retain this mission, it should do so on the full understanding that it will use its division-wing team, not as an amphibious unit, but as a land-based force.

Types of Power Projection

If the Norwegian contingency does not create a legitimate demand for amphibious lift and carrier battle groups, other contingencies certainly do. They also raise three issues: first, the kind of aircraft carriers needed; second, the sophistication of their escorts; and third, the amount of amphibious lift (measured in brigades) and the number of carrier battle groups needed to give high confidence of achieving mission objectives.

At least the first of these issues can be resolved independently of specific planning contingencies. The debate over aircraft carrier size (and propulsion) has continued for many years. Throughout that time the carrier adherents in the Navy have fought for large decks and nuclear propulsion, even though the cost of a Nimitz-class carrier now exceeds $3.5 billion. Critics of these 91,500-ton behemoths have argued at various times for conventionally powered "jeep" carriers with vertical takeoff and landing (VTOL) aircraft—perhaps along the lines of the Soviet Kiev-class carriers, only smaller—and for mid-size decks and fossil-fuel propulsion similar to but more modern than the U.S. Midway class.

The jeep carriers were seen as possible escorts for convoys and as useful instruments in operations against relatively minor threats in ill-defined third-world contingencies. The mid-size carriers would presumably perform the same functions as the large decks, but the argument has been that there could be more of them for the same price. Consequently, an equal or greater number of aircraft could be spread over more decks, the decks themselves could be in more places at one time, and more aircraft would survive enemy attacks because of this dispersal.

In retrospect, none of these arguments seems persuasive. Jeep carriers had a role to play in World War II, when land-based patrol aircraft were limited in range and loiter time and escorts were too small to carry aircraft with them. Now, however, the P-3C patrol aircraft, with a minimal dependence on foreign bases, can cover the key sea-lanes, and modern destroyers and frigates can carry LAMPS (light airborne multi-purpose system) helicopters to provide equivalent protection in the immediate vicinity of convoys. Furthermore, VTOL aircraft are expensive to buy and maintain, are limited in combat radius, and are poor in payload.

Mid-size carriers would be better. But they are not able to handle the Navy's most modern jets and cannot carry the valuable E-2C early warning aircraft, a capability that the British sorely missed in the Falklands. Moreover, if the Navy is correct in its analyses, the cost of aircraft carriers is not directly proportional to their size. Consequently, two mid-size carriers could not be acquired for the price of one large deck. In any event (as table 8-2 shows), the carrier itself, on the average, represents only about 15 percent of the battle group's cost. The aircraft, the escorts, and the underway replenishment ships (UNREPs) account for the bulk of the investment. Mid-size carriers could, at considerable risk, forgo much of the protection that goes with the large decks; VTOL aircraft might miraculously become cheaper to buy and operate than their CTOL (conventional takeoff and landing) counterparts. But short of these changes, it is doubtful that the slightly increased number of carriers would compensate for the disadvantages in performance.

Admittedly, the Navy does not need to buy carrier battle groups on the assumption that all of them would have to operate simultaneously in such "high threat" areas as the north Norwegian Sea and the Sea of Japan. But that is as true of large decks as of mid-size carriers. Although the Navy is understandably concerned about the proliferation of air-to-surface missiles—witness the use of Exocets by Argentina against the British during the battle for the Falkland Islands—this does not mean that it has to acquire the large antimissile capability that it currently plans to do with with the Aegis-equipped cruisers (CG-47s) and destroyers (DDG-51s). A modification of these plans is almost surely in order considering that the amount spent on protecting the carrier already exceeds the cost of the carrier and its offensive capability.

Still more important is the number of carrier battle groups and amphibious brigades the United States should have available. Most critics of large carriers simply argue that small carriers are better and avoid indicating how many of them would be enough. However, in a world of finite resources and many competing claims, force planners cannot avoid the issue. And the Navy does not either. Its position is clear. It has a "requirement"—indeed, it has had a "requirement" since World War II, regardless of changing conditions and circumstances— for 15 large-deck aircraft carriers. The amphibious "requirement," by contrast, has changed. It used to be enough lift for the assault echelons of 2 Marine divisions; now it stands at about 4 brigades (or 1⅓ divisions). Even if the objectives of *The Maritime Strategy* were taken seriously, however, the document provides no specific, contingency-related justification for either capability. This absence leads to the lurking suspicion that, although the Navy is almost certainly right about wanting to retain amphibious forces and large-deck carrier battle groups, it is almost certainly wrong about how many it should have.

Overseas Enemy Bases

Since the Soviet Union seems determined to get into the business of real aircraft carriers (as distinguished from the Moskva and Kiev classes), the Navy could argue that it needs some number of carrier battle groups to hedge against that buildup. But the argument hardly justifies 15 carrier battle groups at this time and fails to support any amphibious brigades at all. Moreover, as the Navy knows and fears, carriers can be attacked with land-based forces. There is no law that requires Soviet carriers to be attacked with U.S. carriers, however much the Navy might wish otherwise.

There are, however, two types of contingencies against which the United States should hedge with a combination of carrier battle groups and amphibious forces. The first would arise if the Soviet navy acquired overseas bases that it would be allowed to convert into the equivalent of home ports and defend with its own forces. The second would arise if the United States, in relation to any of its main force planning contingencies, had to conduct a forced landing operation outside the range of its land-based power, as the British did in recapturing the Falkland Islands. Both types of contingencies would bring the power projection capabilities of the Navy into action.

One can, of course, argue that no independent country, however close its ties to the Soviet Union, would allow the Soviet navy to violate its sovereignty by establishing what would amount to a Soviet bastion on its soil. Unfortunately, the United States cannot be sure that national pride is without price. Concern about the development of Cienfuegos in Cuba as a base for Soviet submarines continues to this day, twenty-five years after the Cuban missile crisis, and with reason. The Soviets have tested periodically to see how far they could go in using and improving the base, presumably with Castro's agreement, without provoking a strong U.S. response. Somalia and Egypt both provided facilities to Soviet ships before they broke their ties with the Soviet Union. South Yemen continues to allow the Soviet navy to use the port of Aden, and Vietnam makes both Cam Ranh Bay and Danang available to Soviet ships and aircraft. Similar developments could occur along the west coast of Africa.

A next step in one or more of these places could easily be the construction of major support facilities and hardened submarine pens as well as the stationing of a brigade or more of Soviet infantry (such as already exists in Cuba), Soviet fighters, and Soviet surface-to-air missiles. With facilities such as these at its disposal, the Soviet navy might risk relocating a portion of its attack submarines outside the area defense barriers the United States would establish in the Atlantic and Pacific in the event of war. This, in turn, could seriously reduce the U.S. Navy's ability to protect essential shipping.

It would pay the United States to prevent these developments from occurring. But there is no assurance that other countries will follow the example of Egypt and Somalia, however rude and demanding the Soviets prove as guests. Hedges against that kind of "breakout" by the Soviet navy therefore seems desirable. The Air Force, with its long-range bombers, could reach these bases despite their remoteness. But whether the bombers could put well-designed submarine pens and support facilities out of action is open to question. There is, in any event, some doubt whether they would be available. The newer heavy bombers, such as the B-1B and ATB (if produced), are likely to be very expensive, few in number, and dedicated to their strategic missions in the event of a major international crisis. What remains of the older B-52 fleet could also have other tasks to occupy it. In these circumstances it would be up to the Navy not only to attack the bases but also to occupy them long enough to destroy or incapacitate their facilities.

Exactly how many amphibious forces and carrier battle groups would be needed for an assault on one of these bases is bound to be uncertain, precisely because the contingency, however dangerous and plausible, remains for the moment hypothetical. However, a preliminary estimate suggests that if the Soviet Union were to defend Cam Ranh Bay with 4 battalions of its naval infantry, 50 bombers, and an air defense system consisting of 72 fighters and 100 surface-to-air missiles, the United States would need a brigade of Marines and 3 carrier battle groups to gain high confidence of overcoming these defenses and disabling the facilities (see table 8-3). If the assault force seems modest in size, one should remember that Soviet battalions are small, a U.S. Marine brigade consists of more than 13,000 men, and 3 large-deck carriers could generate almost as many sorties a day as 3 Air Force fighter wings. Including a battleship in the amphibious force would allow for heavy gunfire support as well.

Assault forces of about the same size would probably be needed to ensure similar confidence of success against other bases. Thus what would determine the amount of amphibious lift and the number of carrier battle groups allocated to this mission would depend on how many such contingencies the United States should be prepared to deal with simultaneously. Since sea control in the Atlantic and Pacific is likely to remain the primary responsibility of the Navy, it would seem prudent to retain the capability to attack simultaneously a base in each ocean. Such an

Table 8-3. U.S. Amphibious Assault on an Enemy Position[a]

Case	Percent of U.S. force surviving	Days to enemy destruction	Days to enemy's probable surrender[b]
A. 2 carrier battle groups and 1 Marine amphibious brigade	84	22.7	10.3
B. 3 carrier battle groups and 1 Marine amphibious brigade[c]	93	14.5	6.6
C. 4 carrier battle groups and 1 Marine amphibious brigade[c]	97	9.2	4.2
D. 4 carrier battle groups and 2 Marine amphibious brigades[c]	99	5.1	2.3

Sources: Table 8-5; and author's estimates.

a. Enemy forces are constant at 50 bombers, 72 fighter and attack aircraft, 100 surface-to-air missiles, and 4 battalions of mechanized infantry.

b. Defined as a loss by the enemy of 40 percent of its ground forces after the Marines have landed.

c. The efficient force could launch three simultaneous attacks, each with 3 CVBGs and 1 MAB; the Navy force could do likewise, but two attacks could contain 4 CVBGs and 1 MAB, while one could include 4 CVBGs and 2 MABs.

attack, which would presumably occur at the beginning of a major ASW campaign, would involve a total ready force of 2 Marine amphibious brigades (36 amphibious ships, 14 escorts, 20 minesweepers, and 2 battleships) as well as 6 carrier battle groups. Since the carrier battle groups might not all be ready for action at any one time, a total of 8 would probably have to be kept in the inventory to maintain 6 on station in wartime.

The Persian Gulf

A Soviet attempt to control the oil states of the Persian Gulf by military means is another important contingency for which amphibious forces and carrier battle groups might prove indispensable. Admittedly, the United States could finance a major synthetic oil industry and put it on a standby basis (with regular modernization and testing) for the investment and operating costs of several new carrier battle groups. Moreover, such a program, even though it would not meet the test of the marketplace, would contribute at least as much to national security as the 3 carrier battle groups forgone. One can argue, however, that the U.S. interest in the Persian Gulf derives as much from the desire to deter aggression and keep the oil fields out of Soviet hands as from the

Table 8-4. Combat Forces Earmarked for the U.S. Central Command[a]

Service and type	Number
Army	
Airborne division	1
Airmobile–air assault division	1
Mechanized infantry division	1
Infantry division	2
Marine Corps	
Marine amphibious force[b]	1⅓
Air Force	
Tactical fighter wing[c]	7
Strategic bomber squadron (B-52)	2
Navy	
Carrier battle group	3
Surface action group	1
Maritime air patrol squadron[d]	5

Source: *Department of Defense Annual Report, Fiscal Year 1987*, p. 272.

a. Although these forces are described as being initially available to USCENTCOM, that would be true only if no other major contingency had previously occurred.

b. A Marine amphibious force typically consists of a reinforced Marine division, a support group, and a Marine air wing (containing roughly twice as many tactical aircraft as an Air Force fighter wing as well as a helicopter unit).

c. Typically 72 fighter and attack aircraft.

d. Usually consists of 9 P-3 long-range antisubmarine warfare aircraft.

objective of retaining access to them for Europe, Japan and, to a lesser extent, the United States itself.

Whatever the future direction of U.S. policy on these issues, both the Carter and Reagan administrations, and to a considerable degree their predecessors, made the decision to keep the oil fields in more or less friendly hands, by deterrence if possible, by force if necessary. One outgrowth of that choice has been the establishment of what was originally known as the rapid deployment force but is now called more modestly the U.S. Central Command (USCENTCOM). Another off-shoot has been the development of an infrastructure to support the rapid movement and supply of U.S. land-based forces designated for (but not solely dedicated to) possible theaters of operation in Southwest Asia, the Middle East, and North Africa.

Table 8-4 lists the forces that would initially be available to USCENT-COM, presumably on the condition that a crisis in Europe had not already swallowed up most of them. A noteworthy part of the list is 3 carrier battle groups, 1 surface action group (a battleship and its escorts), 5 maritime patrol air squadrons (45 aircraft), and 1⅓ Marine amphibious forces, consisting of 4 brigades and their tactical air support. Equally noteworthy, but not on the list, are 13 maritime pre-positioning ships on station in the Indian Ocean with the equipment and supplies for at least 1 Marine Corps brigade. What is not clear is whether all the amphibious lift programmed by the Navy would be committed to USCENTCOM.

Whether because of the usual interservice burden sharing or because of prudent planning, the presence of at least some of these naval forces is a sensible precaution. Unlike the infrastructure for Europe, the one leading into the Persian Gulf area is distant and cannot be considered reliable. Indeed, just when the United States might want to use bases in Africa and the Middle East, some of the host countries could conceivably deny access to them. In the circumstances, as long as the Persian Gulf remains a key contingency for force planning purposes, it makes sense to have a way of establishing a lodgment in the area that will permit the subsequent buildup of land-based forces arriving by air and sea. Carrier battle groups and Marine amphibious units provide just such an alternative to the current base structure.

Exactly where these forces might strike, and against what kind of opposition, is bound to be uncertain. For force planning purposes, however, it seems reasonable to provide for another 4 carrier battle groups (with 3 on station and 1 in overhaul or training during the war) and the amphibious lift for 1 Marine amphibious brigade. This force should prove sufficient to overcome any initial opposition and establish a perimeter large enough to allow airlifted or sealifted reinforcements to enter the area. Indeed, if previous calculations are roughly correct, this combination of sea-based air and ground forces would have at least a 50 percent probability of overcoming as many as 6 Soviet-type battalions and an air defense system consisting of 144 fighters and 200 surface-to-air missiles. Furthermore, the attacking force should be capable of establishing a firm lodgment with a strong defensive perimeter, as well as local air superiority, before major enemy reinforcements could attempt to engage it.

The Southern Flank of NATO

Are there other unique tasks for the power projection forces to perform? The Navy would certainly contend that it has a commitment to provide air support to the NATO allies of the southern flank (principally Greece and Turkey) from the carrier battle groups of the Sixth Fleet and ground reinforcements from Marine amphibious units. But it is unclear whether the Navy sought this commitment to justify its forces in the Mediterranean or whether SACEUR actually requested it. In any event, the commitment does not bind the United States for more than a year at a time.

Furthermore, there are several reasons why the burden of the commitment should be shifted elsewhere. To provide the contemplated support, the Sixth Fleet would have to operate in the eastern Mediterranean, within easy reach of Soviet land-based air power. Many naval officers regard that exposure not simply as sailing in harm's way but as taking on a sea of troubles. Instead of exposing scarce carrier decks to these troubles, it would make a good deal more sense to reinforce the Greeks and Turks with additional land-based support, assuming, of course, that they are not fighting each other and that help is needed.

Italy, which faces little immediate direct threat from the forces of the Warsaw Pact, particularly with Yugoslavia as a buffer, could provide some of the necessary support. So could Spain, as part of its Mediterranean responsibilities. Alternatively, Greece and Turkey could be given greater assistance in the modernization of their own forces, provided they could settle their major differences.

None of these measures would preclude the Sixth Fleet from maintaining a peacetime presence in the Mediterranean if that continues to be deemed desirable. One or more of the substitute measures would, however, be more efficient than adding carrier battle groups and amphibious lift for wartime operations in the eastern Mediterranean.

The contingency of an attack by the Warsaw Pact on NATO's southern flank is important and plausible enough to serve as a basis for allied force planning. Whether, after forty years, it still justifies a large commitment by the United States is open to question. Whether the commitment should be met by carrier battle groups and amphibious forces raises even more serious reservations. Indeed, considering the other available options, it hardly justifies adding 3 more carrier battle groups and the lift for another Marine brigade to the 12 battle groups and 3 brigades of lift warranted by other contingencies.

Power Projection Forces

In sum, a strong case continues to exist for power projection forces in connection with a major antisubmarine warfare campaign and in cases

Table 8-5. Efficient Force Power Projection Capabilities, Fiscal Year 1997
Billions of fiscal 1987 dollars

System	Annual investment, operating and support cost
Carrier battle groups	
12 aircraft carriers (7 with nuclear power; 5 with conventional power)	5.4
12 aircraft wings	10.6[a]
20 CG-47 guided-missile cruisers with Aegis[b]	3.3
8 CGN guided-missile cruisers (with nuclear power)	2.0
27 DDGX guided-missile destroyers with modified Aegis[b]	3.4
4 DDG-993 guided-missile destroyers	0.5
13 DD-963 antisubmarine warfare destroyers	1.7
24 SSN-688 attack submarines (with nuclear power)	3.7
51 underway replenishment ships	2.1
40 FFG-7 guided missile frigates	1.4
Total (199 ships)	34.1
Amphibious forces	
5 LHA amphibious assault ships (with a helicopter deck)	0.8
7 LPH helicopter landing platforms	0.6
11 LPD dock transport ships	0.9
5 LSD dock landing ships	0.2
5 LKA amphibious cargo ships	0.2
20 LST tank landing ships	0.6
2 LCC amphibious command ships	0.1
3 BB battleships with guns and cruise missiles	0.4
9 DD-963 antisubmarine warfare destroyers	0.8
9 FFG-7 guided-missile frigates	0.3
25 MCM, MSH mine countermeasures ships	0.3
Total (101 ships)	5.2

Sources: Table 5-3; *Department of Defense Annual Report, Fiscal Year 1987*, p. 183; and author's estimates.
a. Does not include a share of the cost of training and support aircraft.
b. Aegis is a combination of phased-array radar and battle management system designed to deal with the air threat, including cruise missiles.

where U.S. land-based forces might not be able or allowed to deploy. On the conservative planning assumption that, in wartime, carrier battle groups and Marine amphibious units might have to undertake three more or less simultaneous operations—for planning purposes, two against overseas enemy bases and one to force a lodgment in proximity to advancing enemy forces—the total capability would add up to 12 carrier battle groups and the amphibious lift for 3 Marine brigades (see table 8-5). Should these kinds of contingencies not materialize, but an unforeseen crisis should arise outside the reach of land-based forces, the Navy, with this capability, could concentrate as many as 9 carrier battle groups and a full Marine amphibious force to deal with it.

That would constitute an impressive amount of striking power, especially since, according to the secretary of the navy, modern carriers have as much as eight times the firepower of their World War II predecessors.[1] Certainly it seems sufficient for force planning purposes, considering that neither carrier battle groups nor amphibious forces have a direct role to play in protecting the sea-lanes, and that neither north Norway nor Thrace provides adequate justification for increments to this enormously expensive capability.

Since, in so many of these cases, cheaper and equally effective land-based forces would be or could be made available, the $64 billion dollar questions remains. Why, other than for reasons of comfort, and because they are always nice to have, does the Navy insist on adding 3 more carrier battle groups and the amphibious lift for another Marine brigade to a fleet that will have difficulty enough finding the resources to sustain itself without them in the lean years ahead?

1. See Admiral James D. Watkins, U.S. Navy, *The Maritime Strategy* (Annapolis: U.S. Naval Institute, 1986), p. 34.

CHAPTER NINE

COMMAND OF THE SEAS

THE DOCUMENT *The Maritime Strategy* certainly does not afford a serious justification for more carriers and amphibious lift. The notion that, with 15 carriers and 4 Marine brigades, the U.S. Navy can storm into the Black Sea and refight the Crimean War, or bring the Soviet empire to its knees by raids along the coast of Siberia, is evidence enough of that. But must it be assumed that because of the arguments contained in *The Maritime Strategy,* the Navy's motives are suspect? Or is there something else at work here that makes it so urgent for the Navy to acquire these forces?

Naval Superiority

Admiral Watkins, in *The Maritime Strategy,* denies that the Navy would lead an immediate charge against the Kola Peninsula despite his advocacy of a forward strategy for the fleet.[1] But it is well to remember that Secretary of Defense Weinberger, in one of his earlier incarnations, advocated hitting the Soviet Union at one of its weak points in response to Soviet aggression,[2] and that naval officers, whether or not they have read Mahan and Corbett, have been nurtured in the belief that the first duty of a naval power is to seek command of the seas. Indeed, command of the seas is to the Navy what counterforce and air superiority are to the Air Force.

It is difficult, in principle, to quarrel with the objective of either service. In the case of naval warfare, a considerable body of historical

1. Admiral James D. Watkins, U.S. Navy, *The Maritime Strategy* (Annapolis: U.S. Naval Institute, 1986), pp. 10, 12.
2. *Defense Department Annual Report, Fiscal Year 1983,* p. I-16.

evidence testifies to the advantages of destroying the enemy fleet (which is what command of the seas is all about) and thereby gaining safety for friendly shipping and much greater freedom for the subsequent use of naval power against various targets. The Navy eventually produced this kind of result in the Pacific in World War II, and the allies achieved enough of it in the Atlantic to undertake the Normandy landings without any naval interference from the Germans. The Navy might obtain something of the same result against the Soviet Union if the Soviet fleet, like the Japanese, were to come out and fight in what would probably be a series of losing battles.

Current Problems

But what if the Soviet fleet operated as the German fleet did in World War I, never quite allowing the British to engage it fully except at Jutland, keeping it in being, tying down a large part of British seapower? Some admirals in the Royal Navy had argued before the war that traditional policy should be followed and that the German fleet should be attacked even if it meant dashing into the German home waters to do so. Cooler heads prevailed, and the British instituted what amounted to a long-range blockade of Germany and its fleet in World War I and again in World War II.

Much has changed since then. Carriers are equipped with longer-range, higher-performance aircraft capable of carrying greater loads of ordnance, and carriers themselves have grown tougher, although explosions on the deck can put them out of action for hours or days. Intelligence about the enemy and his movements is likely to be good, though unlikely to improve on the data from the breaking of the German Enigma codes in World War II. Weapons have grown smarter and better able to home in on targets, even when they are moving. But there is the other side of the coin, too. Carriers would probably find it more difficult now to come within range of Soviet home ports without having been detected well in advance. And, to take the Kola Peninsula as an example, Soviet bombers and attack aircraft could conceivably reach the carriers before the carrier-based aircraft could come within range of their targets. This combination of circumstances means not only that the Soviets could begin attacking the U.S. fleet before it could strike back, but also that they could disperse their own ships in different ways, concentrate more aircraft in the area,

Table 9-1. Forces Surviving from Attacks on the Kola Peninsula by U.S. Carrier Battle Groups

Carrier battle groups committed	United States				Soviet Union				
	Carriers	Surface combatants	Fighter aircraft	Attack submarines	Surface combatants	Attack submarines[a]	Surface-to-air missiles	Fighters	Bombers
0	0	0	0	0	100	94	1,000	415	100
3	0	0	0	0	95	93	952	395	95
4	0	0	0	0	91	92	912	379	91
5	0	0	0	0	86	91	859	357	86
6	0	0	0	0	79	90	789	328	79
7	0	0	0	0	70	88	698	290	70
8	0	0	0	0	57	85	574	238	57
9	0	0	0	0	39	82	389	162	39
10	2	17	153	4	0	74	0	0	0
11	5	40	364	10	0	74	0	0	0
12	7	56	501	14	0	74	0	0	0

Source: Author's estimates.

a. It is assumed that out of 141 attack submarines, 47 are on their way to attack U.S. shipping, 20 are available to attack the carrier battle groups, and 74 are in submarine pens that cannot be destroyed by conventional ordnance.

and deploy some portion of their attack submarines along the route of the battle groups. Under such conditions the carriers would risk serious damage, yet might not find much of a target system to strike for all their pains. The effect on the campaign for control of the sea-lanes would be minimal, and fewer carriers would be left for other critical missions.

Favorable Conditions

That is perhaps the worst case. Suppose, however, that more favorable conditions prevail. In a less demanding contingency, the Soviets commit the attack submarines in the Northern Fleet to immediate raids on the North Atlantic shipping lanes in such a way that 47 of them are out of port and on their way to their stations. The remaining 94 attack submarines are in port, but 20 of them are able to move out to intercept the carriers, given a day of warning. All Soviet surface combatants are also in port, and only the normal complement of bombers and fighters is available. Because the weather is poor and the carrier battle groups use excellent tactics of concealment and deception, the Soviet commander obtains just enough warning of their approach to get 20 submarines under way, put his 100 surface combatants and 1,000 SAMs on antiaircraft alert, and launch 100 bombers and 415 fighters. By the time these actions have occurred, the carrier-based attack aircraft come within range of their targets.

Exactly how successful the U.S. attack would be under these conditions depends on several factors. Table 9-1 shows the expected number of ships sunk and aircraft lost on each side as a function of the number of carrier battle groups committed to the attack by the United States. If the U.S. Navy has a total inventory of 15 carriers, as planned, but with 9 of them occupied on other vital missions, the 3 available for the Kola attack will make a very small dent in Soviet naval capabilities and, on the average, all the carriers will be lost.

If 5 of the 15 carriers are allocated to the Second Fleet, as suggested in *The Maritime Strategy,* perhaps as many as 4 could join in the attack. Although they would cause somewhat greater damage to the Soviet fleet and its aircraft, all 4 of them would also be lost. Moreover, only 8 carriers would be available for such other contingencies as enemy overseas ports and the Persian Gulf. However, if 10 carriers were committed to the attack, the tide would turn in favor of the United States in the sense that at least 2 carriers would survive, while Soviet surface combatants and naval aviation in the area would be decimated. In the process, unfortunately, so would be the ability of the Navy to undertake other major missions with its carriers.

Perhaps these losses could be deemed acceptable if such an attack gave the United States and its allies genuine command of the Atlantic. But that does not appear to be what happens. Admittedly, for the price of 8 carriers and a number of escorts, the attack gets rid of the Soviet surface combatants and bombers. But these results, arguably, are disappointingly small compared with the costs. Neither of these enemy forces represents the major threat to the sea-lanes; both can be countered by land-based aircraft and the barrier forces the Navy would put into place in any event. Thus the two main potential benefits would come from facilitating to some degree a U.S. attempt to sink Soviet SSBNs with attack submarines, and from reducing the submarine threat to the Atlantic sea-lanes.

Carrier Raids and ASW

No one knows whether a president would even authorize an attack on Soviet SSBNs in these circumstances. What seems more evident is that the carrier raids are not an efficient way to reduce the submarine threat to allied shipping. It is worth recalling in this connection that of the 141 attack submarines in the Soviet Northern Fleet, 47 were assumed to be allocated to attacks on the sea-lanes, another 20 to attacks on the carrier battle groups, while the remaining 74 were left in port. Because of this distribution, and the hardness of the submarine pens in port, the carrier raid itself does not inflict great losses on the Soviet attack submarines, although the losses grow as the size of the raid increases. Consequently, the main threat to allied control of the Atlantic diminishes but does not disappear.

Still, the carrier raid does reduce the amount of damage the Soviet submarines can do to U.S. shipping and thereby increases the amount of tonnage delivered to U.S. forces in Europe. Furthermore, as assumptions are changed and the Soviets hold more of their submarines in home waters, more of them get sunk, and the carriers also fare less well, but more tonnage arrives in Europe (see table 9-2).

At first glance, these results may seem to justify both the carrier raid

Table 9-2. Tonnage Delivered to Europe as the Soviet Union Allocates More Submarines to Attack Ten Carrier Battle Groups

				5 convoys per month	
Case	Soviet submarines allocated to Atlantic sea-lanes[a]	Soviet submarines allocated to carrier battle groups	Percent of 10 carrier battle groups lost	U.S. ships lost in first four months	Millions of tons delivered to Europe in first four months
1	67	0	73	153	18.47
2	47	20	79	106	18.49
3	37	30	82	83	19.17
4	27	40	86	62	19.38
5	17	50	93	39	19.61
6	12	60	100	27	19.73

Sources: Table 7-2; and author's estimates.
a. It is assumed that there are 141 attack submarines in the Soviet Northern Fleet (as shown in table 6-1). Of these, 74 are in port in hardened submarine pens. In case 1, all 67 of the remainder attack the Atlantic sea-lanes, as assumed in table 7-2. In successive cases, the USSR allocates fewer of them to the antishipping campaign and more to the anticarrier battle. As a consequence, more U.S. warships are sunk, but more U.S. shipping reaches Europe.

and an increased number of carrier battle groups, despite their impressive investment and operating costs. However, in analysis as in life, first impressions may be misleading. Even with a total inventory of 15 carriers, of which 12, on the average, would be available for action, an early and moderately effective attack on the Kola Peninsula would absorb so many of them that the Navy would have to delay or forgo other vital missions. And it would certainly lack the capacity to undertake a similar raid against Vladivostok and Petropavlovsk.

Of course, one can argue, in spite of the assumption of *The Maritime Strategy,* that future conflicts on land and at sea will be limited in scope rather than worldwide, that an attack in Central Europe could be confined to the Atlantic area, and that the Soviet Union would lack the capability to circumvent the U.S. area ASW defenses. In these circumstances might it not pay the Navy to risk a large number of its carriers against the Kola Peninsula while retaining a few in reserve for other contingencies?

Such a scenario is at least as plausible as the one presented in *The Maritime Strategy.* Moreover, if the carriers are treated as a sunk cost and the scenario is considered in isolation, the payoff may seem worth the risk. But from the standpoint of force planning, three questions still remain. First, could other forces conduct the raid at lower cost and about equal effectiveness? Second, are there no other ways to achieve the same effect on the battle of the sea-lanes at lower cost? Third, would not a raid on Soviet territory, however conducted, and especially if it coincided with attacks on Soviet SSBNs, cause negative reactions within the alliance and greatly increase the probability that the war would escalate to the disaster of a nuclear exchange?

Evaluating the Options

The first two questions are easier to answer than the third. One reason for justifying the use of carrier battle groups to execute the raid—assuming the contingency itself could be justified in the first place—is that there might be no other choice. In the event, allies such as Norway and Great Britain might deny the use of their bases for attacks by land-based aircraft on the ground that it would be too provocative. Indeed, problems in 1986 with the use of F-111s in the raid on Libya lend credence to this concern and suggest that the allies might even persuade the president to forgo the raid altogether.

However, even if allies refused the use of their bases for this purpose and rejected the idea of the raid itself, the United States could still conduct it with a combination of long-range bombers, attack submarines, and various modern mines. Just as B-52s or wide-bodied aircraft equipped with cruise missiles can engage in maritime patrol and search for enemy ships, so can they reach the Kola Peninsula and do as much damage to the surface combatants and aircraft of the Northern Fleet as the carrier battle groups. For their part, attack submarines armed with torpedoes and mines could make life as difficult for Soviet submarines as the carriers.

This combination is also cheaper than 3 new carrier battle groups. As can be seen from table 9-3, 72 bombers, with a total payload equal to that of all the fighter and attack aircraft on 3 carriers, together with 6 attack submarines of the Los Angeles class, could be acquired for $33.9 billion, $20.7 billion less than the cost of the 3 additional battle groups. For equal cost, a mixture of 98 bombers and 18 attack submarines could be deployed, enough to run substantial raids on both the Northern and the Pacific fleets. To minimize interservice rivalries, the secretary of defense could even allow the Navy to buy and operate the bombers.

Another option—one the Navy would probably find more palatable—is to buy more ASW capability. *The Maritime Strategy* makes the

Table 9-3. Trade-offs between Carrier Battle Groups and B-1B–SSN Combinations
Costs in billions of 1987 dollars

System and type of trade-off	Delivery systems	Available weapons	Weapons delivered	Acquistion cost
Carrier battle groups (3)	...	...	...	**54.6**
Aircraft	216	3,240	648	...
Submarines	6	120	30	...
B-1B–SSNs (equal effectiveness)	...	...	...	**33.9**
B-1Bs[a]	72	3,240	648	21.6
Tankers	72	...	...	7.2
SSNs[b]	6	120	30	5.1
B-1B–SSNs (equal cost)	...	...	...	**54.5**
B-1Bs[a]	98	4,410	882	29.4
Tankers	98	...	...	9.8
SSNs[b]	18	360	90	15.3
Carrier battle groups (10)	...	...	...	**182.0**
Aircraft	720	10,800	2,160	...
Submarines	20	400	100	...
B-1B–SSNs (equal effectiveness)	...	...	...	**113.0**
B-1Bs[a]	240	10,800	2,160	72.0
Tankers	240	...	...	24.0
SSNs[b]	20	400	100	17.0
B-1B–SSNs (equal cost)	...	...	...	**182.0**
B-1Bs[a]	370	16,650	3,330	111.0
Tankers	370	...	...	37.0
SSNs[b]	40	800	200	34.0

Sources: Table 8-2; and author's estimates.
a. Air Force heavy bombers. A cheaper long-range cruise-missile carrier (CMC) based on a wide-bodied commercial aircraft would also be an option.
b. Nuclear-powered attack submarines of the Los Angeles class (SSN-688).

necessary bow to the importance of ASW, but its main purpose is to justify the Navy's power projection forces. It is little wonder, therefore, that its authors make much of their forward strategy and emphasize how the amphibious forces and carrier battle groups will win the war. The mundane truth, however, is that the main mission of the Navy is to keep the sea-lanes open to the overseas land theaters where the decisive battles will be deterred or fought. Thus if more tonnage needs to be saved on the way to these theaters, which is debatable, it can be saved much more efficiently with increments of standard ASW than with additional carriers and raids on Soviet home ports.

Admittedly, only so much can be done to strengthen further the main area barriers. But open-ocean search can always be expanded with a combination of towed array ships and patrol aircraft, and the number of escorted convoys can be increased enough to ensure delivery of the

Table 9-4. Trading Carrier Battle Groups for Convoys and Escorts (Atlantic)
Tonnage in millions

Carrier battle groups (CVBGs)	Soviet SSNs attacking sea-lanes	Soviet SSNs attacking CVBGs	Tonnage delivered in four months	Additional tonnage delivered in four months	Equal cost Convoyed ships	Escorts	Tonnage delivered in four months	Additional tonnage delivered in four months
...	67[a]	...	18.47[a]	...	500[a]	50[a]	18.47[a]	...
3	47	20	18.49	0.02	687	68	25.95[b]	7.48
4	37	30	19.17	0.70	749	74	28.43	9.96
5	27	40	19.38	0.91	811	81	30.91	12.44
6	17	50	19.61	1.14	873	87	34.92	16.45
7	7	60	19.85	1.38	936	93	35.91	17.44
8	0	67	20.00[b]	1.53	998[c]	99[c]	38.39[c]	19.92[c]

Sources: Tables 7-2, 8-2; and author's estimates.
a. This is the base case. The Navy would buy this capability regardless of whether the CVBGs attacked the Kola Peninsula.
b. When all the Soviet SSNs are diverted to attacking the CVBGs, additional ships and escorts are a better buy than 3 CVBGs (at $54.6 billion).
c. For the price of 8 CVBGs, it would be possible to buy enough loaded ships and escorts to duplicate virtually the original 500 ships and 50 escorts.

same amount of tonnage as would get through if carrier raids took place. This last possibility for substitution is examined in table 9-4. As can be seen, without any raids and without any addition to the baseline number of 5 escorted U.S. convoys in the Atlantic, the Navy could deliver nearly 18.5 million tons of supplies to Europe during the first four months of the campaign. That is enough to keep U.S. ground and tactical air forces in Europe at full combat power, assuming always that forty-five days' worth of stocks had been pre-positioned in the theater and that the enemy had not destroyed more than nine days of supply. A raid on the Kola Peninsula by 3 carrier battle groups would perhaps increase this four-month delivery by as much as 20,000 tons, or less than 1 percent. For the cost of the 3 battle groups, enough transport ships, cargoes, and escorts could be bought to deliver nearly 7.5 million tons more during the same amount of time. Thus although none of the increased ASW capability may be necessary, the fact that it can produce the same results as the carriers, and at much lower cost, is simply another illustration of how inefficient these raids would be and why it is so difficult to understand why the Navy wants or needs 3 more carrier battle groups.

Provocation and Escalation

To doubt the usefulness of maintaining more than 12 carrier battle groups or of attempting to gain command of the seas by raids on Soviet home ports early in a conventional conflict, and to rest those doubts on grounds of cost and effectiveness, may suggest an insensitivity to issues of provocation, instability, and escalation. Such is not the case. Even if, by some magic, the Navy could make the raids so efficient that they would give the United States true command of the seas (and actually reduce or eliminate the need for expensive ASW capabilities), the attacks would still be a bad bargain if they increased the probability of nuclear war from, say, 5 percent to 50 percent, or even a much smaller amount.

It is difficult, however, to demonstrate that the raids by themselves would increase the risk to this or any other degree. The range of uncertainty is wide. It is by no means clear, for example, that the Soviets would interpret the raids, or the Navy's willingness to sink SSBNs as well as attack submarines, in precisely the way many Americans would have them do. No one seriously doubts that much of the Soviets' own ASW effort is directed toward the sinking of U.S. SSBNs, or that the

Soviets would try to destroy NATO's theater-based nuclear weapons with nonnuclear attacks in the event of a conventional war in Europe. It would be surprising, in the circumstances, if they anticipated any different behavior on the part of the United States, or would be any more provoked to nuclear escalation if it did occur.

No one, naturally, can be expected to wax enthusiastic over an attempted attrition of SSBN capabilities. But it has been and remains a fairly safe bet that neither side would want to begin a nuclear exchange over some missing SSBNs, however important they may be to deterrence. If one worries about this kind of provocation, one should probably believe as well that the announced U.S. policy of using nuclear weapons rather than suffering a conventional setback, wherever it might occur, will prove at least as provocative and might serve even more as a triggering event to catastrophe. Yet there is remarkably little concern about that policy.

That the Soviet leadership would see U.S. attacks on Soviet home ports as justifying a nuclear war cannot be taken for granted. If the Soviets had with malice aforethought set out to conquer Europe by conventional means, they could hardly have done so without allowing for a violent reaction by the United States, which, at a minimum, would include air strikes deep into Eastern Europe. To imagine that a conventional attack on the Kola Peninsula, however rashly conceived, would then cause them to change their minds and resort to nuclear weapons is to ascribe a degree of irrationality to them for which no evidence exists.

On the other hand, if the war were to begin, not as a calculated aggression, but as the outgrowth of a crisis in Eastern Europe that had grown unmanageable in the best tradition of the prisoner's dilemma, the attitudes and reactions of the Soviet leadership might be somewhat different. Still, those who see nuclear deterrence as easy to attain and highly shockproof, yet find the potential for nuclear escalation in every military act, seem to want it both ways. Their world consists of solid deterrents easily obtained and fragile stability easily disturbed.

So far, fortunately, the mad automatons that inhabit this peculiar action-reaction model and have eternally itchy fingers on the nuclear trigger, ready to fire at the least provocation, have not yet come to life. In their stead are leaders on both sides who lean toward caution in the face of uncertainty and commit their follies, for the most part, in places such as Cuba, Afghanistan, and Grenada. Kola probably is not such a place, no matter what the Navy may argue. Something of a learning process does go on.

What leaders have learned less well is that military "requirements" are not to be confused with serious and demonstrable military needs. The Navy has just such a serious, demonstrable need, based on specific and worrisome contingencies: it is for 12 carrier battle groups and the amphibious lift for 3 Marine Corps brigades. The Navy also has a "requirement" for 15 carrier battle groups and the lift for 4 Marine Corps brigades. Neither of these latter numbers has more than the general assertions of *The Maritime Strategy* behind it, yet more than $64 billion are at stake. The need has already been met; 12 deployable carrier battle groups and the amphibious lift for a Marine amphibious force are currently in hand. The requirement should be ignored unless the Navy can produce a much more sober case for it than it has done so far.

CHAPTER TEN

SETTING A NEW COURSE

ONLY the leaders of a defeated power can enjoy the luxury of building a navy from scratch. U.S. presidents and their secretaries of defense have not been able to count on that luxury. They have always been saddled with a large inheritance that they could change only over a long period of time.

The Navy is particularly resistant to any such change. It is a complex machine with many moving parts that are not easy to synchronize. Therefore, once meshed and steered on a given course, as the Navy now is toward the golden fleece of 600 ships—or more like 622 to 650, depending on who does the counting—it develops a great forward momentum. A change of course is not easy in these circumstances. Yet the need for a new course is real and the opportunity to set it still exists. If the change is not made voluntarily, the severe constraints on the defense budget in the years ahead (barring always a great international emergency) are likely to force a change anyway, but not necessarily one for the better.

This prospect raises three final questions. What constitutes a Navy capable, with high confidence, of dealing with the basic and plausible contingencies that should be the starting point for force planning? To what extent can the resulting fleet fulfill the peacetime functions that presidents tend to expect of it? And how can the secretary of defense change the Navy's course yet stay within the confines of a defense budget that, while already large, is unlikely to grow in real terms from its fiscal 1986 baseline for the next five years?

Size and Composition

The size and composition of the Navy are supposed to reflect not only the contingencies used for force planning purposes and the missions demanded of it, but also a significant probability that it can reach realistic objectives despite the opposition of an intelligent and uncooperative enemy. As far as such considerations regain some influence in the Department of Defense, the Navy deserves to and should fare well, even though perhaps less well than it would like in a period of static defense budgets.

In the deterrence of strategic nuclear attack, the Navy's role should, if anything, expand. SSBNs are likely to remain the most survivable leg of the strategic Triad despite Soviet efforts to defeat them. With the deployment of the Trident II (D-5) ballistic missile, they will have the capability to execute all the missions that can realistically be asked of the strategic nuclear forces. In every respect, SLBMs will have the advantage over the MX and Midgetman.

In principle, the Navy holds a similar advantage in deterring the tactical use of nuclear weapons, provided it is fully recognized that the capabilities for this purpose should be designed on the same principles and with the same objectives as the strategic nuclear forces. It is by no means clear, however, that the attack submarines currently designated as the main platforms for the TLAM-N should be burdened with this mission as an afterthought to their primary task, which is antisubmarine warfare in a conventional campaign. That problem aside, their utility for theater nuclear deterrence remains in question because the Navy, reportedly, is unwilling to dedicate the TLAM-Ns to targets in Eastern Europe and cannot guarantee that the attack submarines would be within range of these tactical targets when needed. Rather than continue on this course, the Navy might consider whether the older SSBNs of the Madison and Franklin classes, when decommissioned as strategic submarines, should not be converted to cruise missile platforms. With this configuration it could hold them in readiness to attack specific tactical targets as part of a theater nuclear command separate from both the strategic nuclear and the conventional forces. To convert the older Poseidon boats and rework their propulsion systems would certainly cost more than to continue putting the TLAM-N in the bilges of the attack submarines. But the benefits of having a survivable, single-purpose, and controllable capability would outweigh the additional costs.

The major force planning contingencies for conventional war and its deterrence place an equally heavy burden on the Navy. Given these contingencies, it seems conservative but still reasonable for the Navy to deploy large enough forces to perform three main missions: form the key barriers to submarines in the Atlantic and Pacific; handle three

Table 10-1. U.S. Fleet Comparisons, Mid-1990s

Deployable battle force	Navy preferred	Official Department of Defense[a]	Efficient force
SSBNs (ballistic missile submarines)	44	40	41
SSGNs (cruise missile submarines)	. . .	. . . .	7
CVs/CVNs (aircraft carriers)	15	15	12
BBs (battleships)	4	4	3
SSNs (nuclear-powered attack submarines)	100	100	96
CGs, CGNs, DDs, DDGs, FFs, FFGs (surface combatants)[b]	253	238	220
Patrol combatants	. . .	6	. . .
Amphibious ships	74	75	55
Mine warfare ships	31	14	25
Underway replenishment ships	69	65	51
Material and fleet support ships	60	65	60
Total	650	622	570

Sources: Peter T. Tarpgaard, *Building a 600-Ship Navy: Costs, Timing and Alternative Approaches* (Congressional Budget Office, 1982), p. 89; *Department of Defense Annual Report, Fiscal Year 1987*, p. 179; and author's estimates based on tables 3-5, 4-4, 7-2, 7-3, 8-3.

a. This is the high side of the range shown in table 1-4.

b. For the specific designators and their interpretation, see appendix A.

simultaneous but limited contingencies with carrier battle groups and Marine amphibious brigades; and furnish the escorts for nine U.S. convoys a month to Europe, Northeast Asia, and the Persian Gulf. Allied naval forces, for their part, can assume the responsibility for bottling up the Soviet Baltic and Black Sea fleets, keeping open the sea-lanes in the Mediterranean, and protecting their own convoys across the Atlantic and out to 1,000 miles from Japan in the Pacific.

Force Comparisons

The main nuclear and conventional naval forces derived from these force planning contingencies can be listed and compared with the Navy's preferred fleet (see table 10-1). What is called the efficient force is not much smaller than the Navy fleet. But the differences between the two are significant. The efficient force contains 12 rather than 15 deployable carrier battle groups and 3 rather than 4 brigades of amphibious lift for power projection. Because of these changes, it deploys a slightly smaller number of attack submarines, but it also contains more escorts for convoy duty.

Table 10-2. Hypothetical 600-Ship and Efficient Navy Five-Year Plans,
Fiscal Years 1987–91
Billions of fiscal 1987 dollars (with all pay excluded)[a]

	Budget authority					
Item	1987	1988	1989	1990	1991	Total
600-ship Navy	83.7	92.4	97.8	100.0	106.5	480.4
Efficient Navy	78.3	78.3	78.3	78.3	78.3	391.5
Saving	5.4	14.1	19.5	21.7	28.2	88.9

Sources: Peter T. Tarpgaard and Robert E. Mechanic, *Future Budget Requirements for the 600-Ship Navy* (Congressional Budget Office, 1985), p. 68; and author's estimates.

a. All pay is excluded so as to avoid erroneous assumptions about retired pay accrual and the Department of the Navy's share of it. If pay were included, the saving would be larger, since the efficient navy would need fewer personnel.

As a result of these shifts in emphasis, the efficient force requires a less ambitious long-term shipbuilding program than the Navy fleet. Indeed, because so many of the key components of the efficient force have already been funded, and because it does not depend on some of the more expensive new ships and service life extensions planned by the Navy, the secretary of defense can acquire and sustain the efficient force without major contract adjustments and without any real growth in the budget of the Department of the Navy for the next five years (see table 10-2). By contrast, the Navy fleet would require more new ships and annual real growth of more than 3 percent during the same period (as also shown in table 10-2) according to the estimates of the Congressional Budget Office.[1] This increase is almost certainly unrealistic in the era of Gramm-Rudman-Hollings. In any event, it is not needed.

The uniformed Navy, with its sharply honed bureaucratic skills, may yet find a way to rob Peter (also known as the Army and Air Force) to pay Paul and retain its ambitious shipbuilding program despite future constraints on the defense budget. Therefore, it is not without interest to see how the Navy-preferred fleet compares in performance with the efficient force.

The two should perform their nuclear missions on about equal terms, although the efficient force has the advantage of a special and more responsive capability dedicated to nuclear attacks on theater targets. Table 10-3 shows how many targets in the Soviet Union and Eastern Europe the two forces could cover on a second strike and what damage

1. Peter T. Tarpgaard and Robert E. Mechanic, *Future Budget Requirements for the 600-Ship Navy* (Congressional Budget Office, 1985), p. viii, and cost tables A-1, A-2, A-3, pp. 66–68.

Table 10-3. Performance of the Programmed and Efficient Forces on Nuclear Missions, Fiscal Year 1997
Percent

| | Second-strike damage expectancy[a] | | | |
| | Programmed force | | Efficient force | |
Targets	Day-to-day alert	Generated alert	Day-to-day alert	Generated alert
Strategic forces				
1,670 hard strategic	73.7	76.9	74.9	94.2
316 soft strategic	75.3	96.2	80.0	95.9
740 peripheral attack	20.8	82.6	62.0	80.0
410 general purpose forces	46.8	88.5	80.0	82.4
500 logistics and energy	31.2	88.5	80.0	96.0
1,380 urban-industrial	76.4	80.0	76.4	80.0
Overall damage expectancy	60.3	81.9	74.7	87.5
Tactical nuclear forces				
72 airfields	. . .	80.6	. . .	80.6
191 choke points	. . .	80.1	. . .	80.5
162 bunkers	. . .	60.5	. . .	80.2
832 maneuver battalions	. . .	3.1	. . .	83.8
Overall damage expectancy	. . .	26.7	. . .	82.6

Sources: Tables 3-2, 3-6, 4-2, 4-3, 4-4; and author's estimates.
a. Expected percentage of target destroyed. Both forces attack the same 5,016 strategic and 1,257 tactical targets.

expectancies they should be able to achieve. The Navy-preferred force, as far as one can determine it, covers 6,273 targets, with an overall damage expectancy of 59 percent. The efficient force attacks the same number of targets and obtains an overall damage expectancy of 76 percent.

If planners were to take seriously the pretensions of *The Maritime Strategy*, they would find it impossible to compare the Navy fleet with the efficient force in a hypothetical conventional war, since the two forces would supposedly proceed on such different courses. *The Maritime Strategy* would have the Navy fleet mop up those unfortunate Soviet ships that had not already fled to home waters, and then surge forward to bottle up or destroy the main Soviet fleets as a prelude to doing to the Soviet Union what Admirals William F. Halsey, Marc Mitscher, and Raymond A. Spruance did to Japan, and what the Marines did to Iwo Jima and Okinawa (with help from the Army) during World War II.

However, assuming that reason will eventually replace nostalgic rhetoric on these matters, the national command authorities will likely

Table 10-4. Performance of the Programmed and Efficient Forces on Conventional Missions, Fiscal Year 1997

Item	Objective	Programmed force	Efficient force
		Millions of tons	
Tonnage delivered by D-day plus 120			
To Western Europe when			
USSR deploys submarines on D-day	20.0	18.40	22.47
USSR predeploys 20 submarines before D-day	20.0	18.02	22.02
USSR seizes North Norway at D-day	20.0	17.57	21.57
USSR seizes Iceland at D-day	20.0	17.45	21.45
USSR bases submarines in overseas ports	20.0	14.53	18.53
To Northeast Asia and Persian Gulf when			
USSR deploys submarines on D-day	10.0	7.02	11.02
		Percent	
Probability of success in			
Establishing lodgment in Persian Gulf	70.0	87.4[a]	70.3
Destroying two Soviet overseas home ports	70.0	70.3	70.3
Destroying the Soviet Northern Fleet (Kola Peninsula)	70.0	8.6[b]	. . .[c]

Sources: Tables 7-2, 7-3, 8-1, 8-3, 9-1.

a. The programmed force is able to commit 2 Marine amphibious brigades to this attack, while the efficient force can commit only 1.

b. The programmed force commits 3 carrier battle groups to the attack. It would take about 15 carrier battle groups to achieve the desired probability of success.

c. The efficient force does not acquire forces for this mission.

think about the fleet and its utility in much the same way as the hypothetical planners of the efficient force do. This means that they would have at their disposal a somewhat greater capability for power projection with the Navy fleet than with the efficient fleet and a somewhat lesser capability for convoy defenses in the ASW campaign. Because of these differences, the efficient force (as shown in table 10-4) would do better in delivering tonnage to the overseas forces, but take slightly longer to achieve its power projection objectives. However, its ten-year cost would be considerably less (as seen in table 10-2).

Peacetime Presence

Laymen are likely to believe that war, and the deterrence of war by the demonstrated ability to perform wartime missions successfully, are the most important functions of the Navy, especially at the prices being paid for it. But the argument persists that the size and composition of the Navy should be shaped as much, if not more, by its role in what used

Table 10-5. Hypothetical Peacetime Deployments of Navy and Efficient Forces[a]

Type of ship	Second Fleet		Sixth Fleet		Third Fleet		Seventh Fleet		Total	
	Navy	Efficient	Navy	Efficient	Navy	Efficient	Navy	Efficient	Navy	Efficient
Ballistic missile submarines	32	30	...	...	12	11	...	...	44	41
Cruise missile submarines	...	7	...	...	...	...	...	...	...	7
Aircraft carriers	6	5	2	1	5	5	2[b]	1	15	12
Battleships	2	1	...	...	2	2	...	...	4	3
Other surface combatants	109	95	22	19	92	80	30	26	253	220
Nuclear-powered attack submarines	50	48	6	6	36	35	8	7	100	96
Amphibious ships	31	23	8	6	26	19	9	7	74	55
Mine countermeasures ships	13	11	3	2	11	9	4	3	31	25
Underway replenishment ships	28	21	9	5	23	21	9	4	69	51
Auxiliaries	28	28	5	5	21	21	6	6	60	60
Total	299	269	55	44	228	203	65	54	650	570

Sources: *Department of Defense Annual Report, Fiscal Year 1987*, pp. 272, 276; John M. Collins, *U.S.-Soviet Military Balance, 1980–1985* (Washington, D.C.: Pergamon-Brassey's, 1985), p. 146; and author's estimates.
a. The deployed forces are assumed to be averages rather than fixed, steady-state deployments, particularly in the case of the efficient force.
b. One carrier is assumed to be homeported in Japan.

to be called gunboat diplomacy and in peacetime cruises overseas. Fortunately, the Army and the Air Force have not made similar claims to a peacekeeping role, even though they too can wander about overseas. If they did make such claims, the possibilities for increases in the defense budget might become endless. Still, since the Navy seems to have established a corner on that market, and since the demand for the product is strong (especially from agencies that do not have to pay for it), perhaps the best way to consider this demand is to ask whether a fleet designed to deal with serious wartime contingencies is adequate to perform peacetime functions, and whether it is worth the cost to remove alleged deficiencies by buying more ships.

In this connection, since so many misunderstandings exist about force planning methodology, it may be worth repeating why the methodology is unlikely to produce picayune capabilities. First, the planning contingencies are selected on the ground that they would threaten the United States itself or areas and interests of great importance to it. Second, they are designed so that they reflect severe but not unrealistic challenges, since potential enemies are unlikely to be benign and cooperative. Third, the number of contingencies for which the United States should be prepared to act on simultaneously tends to be on the conservative side and, especially when nuclear and naval responses are included, is much higher than such labels as one-and-one-half or two-and-one-half war strategies suggest. Fourth, although the contingencies used for determining force size and composition are intended to help generate the military capabilities necessary to repel the most serious challenges to U.S. security, and at the same time avoid overambitious demands for forces, they are not intended to link the resulting forces solely to particular theaters or functions. In any wartime or peacetime situation, it will be up to the president and his advisers, not the force planners, to determine where and how to deploy and operate these capabilities. At that point, the force planner can only hope that, in the face of multiple uncertainties, he has provided enough tools (but not too many) for the job.

According to *The Maritime Strategy,* the 600-ship navy in peacetime as well as wartime will deploy in four main fleets. Table 10-5 compares these deployments with what the efficient force would be capable of doing under the same conditions and rules about ship rotations in peacetime. Since the efficient force is smaller, it does not keep as many ships on station. But it would be just as capable of conducting a Libyanscale operation as the Navy fleet and, given as much time, could concentrate at least 4 carrier battle groups in response to an emergency, compared with the 5 that the Navy fleet could make available. Despite its somewhat smaller size, the efficient force would have no difficulty in exercising U.S. rights to the freedom of the seas, whether in the Gulf of Sidra, the Black Sea, the Arctic Ocean, or the Sea of Japan. However, because the efficient force contains 3 fewer carriers, 1 less battleship, and 19 fewer amphibious ships, perhaps it could not maintain as imposing a presence overseas from day to day as the Navy's fleet.

Policymakers, especially from the Department of State, have assumed for many years that an established naval presence overseas of a certain size exercises a great influence, and they have resisted any change in it (especially since they are not paying for the presence or even renting it). From time to time, some have gone so far as to assert that a major reduction in the Sixth Fleet in the Mediterranean or the Seventh Fleet in the western Pacific would have catastrophic effects on U.S. friends in those areas.

So far, no one has succeeded in demonstrating what effects, if any, these deployments have had in underwriting U.S. commitments, reassuring allies, or keeping the peace.[2] But events during the past decade have conspired to suggest that changes in the Sixth and Seventh Fleets have not resulted in the predicted consequences. Because of concerns about the situation in the Persian Gulf, American authorities have withdrawn both carrier battle groups and amphibious forces from the Mediterranean and the western Pacific in order to show the flag and establish a presence in the Arabian Sea. Panic did not follow in other areas. And conceivably the allies felt more comfortable with U.S. ships near the sources of their oil supply than in their home waters.

It is worthy of note, in any event, that for at least a decade the Navy contributed whatever it does to international peace and stability with 12 carrier battle groups and 3 Marine amphibious brigades. Taxpayers are therefore entitled to wonder whether the investment of $67 billion in 3 more carrier battle groups, 4 battleships, and an additional Marine amphibious brigade will result in a peacetime improvement commensurate with the costs, especially considering the needs of the other armed forces and of the society as a whole.

Whatever benefits peacetime deployments overseas may confer, ships

2. See Barry M. Blechman and Stephen S. Kaplan, *Force without War: U.S. Armed Forces as a Political Instrument* (Brookings, 1978).

must steam and planes must fly to train and maintain combat effectiveness. Consequently, they may as well practice in waters with which they should become familiar, and in conjunction with allied navies. These activities also increase their understanding of Soviet naval capabilities. As for the cost of overseas exercises in fuel and other consumables, they are not much greater than if the ships steamed and the planes flew the same amount in U.S. home waters.

Nonetheless, a day-to-day overseas presence does exact a price. The Navy likes to portray its carrier battle groups and amphibious forces, accompanied by their underway replenishment groups, as self-sufficient and floating free. However, it maintains a substantial foreign base structure, and the steady overseas presence of the Sixth and Seventh fleets no doubt increases the cost of operating the bases. More important, extended tours of duty at sea, though broken by visits to foreign ports, heighten the already difficult task of manning the Navy's ships and are likely to drive up the cost of retaining existing personnel and enlisting qualified recruits at a time when the pool of eligible volunteers is shrinking. The Navy, in fact, finds itself in a vicious circle. It wants more ships not least because a larger fleet means a more rapid rotation of ships on station overseas and shorter tours of duty at sea for their crews. But, of course, a larger fleet requires higher retention rates and more recruits, and so on.

Selective Presence

One part of a solution to this problem is to settle for the less ambitious goals represented by the efficient force. Another part is to change the alleged requirement for a sustained naval presence overseas. It is important to recognize, in this connection, that the deployment of the Sixth and Seventh fleets was not dictated by some farsighted plan to contain the Soviet Union or by any premeditated U.S. decision to go on world patrol. The Sixth Fleet originally went to the Mediterranean because of the precarious situation in Greece after World War II; the Seventh Fleet remained in the western Pacific, first because of the postwar turmoil in China and then as a barrier between the communist forces on the mainland and Taiwan. Neither fleet was intended as a permanent fixture, although the Navy quickly recognized that if it could retain two sizable fleets on station and establish the principle of having

Table 10-6. U.S. Surface Combatant Steaming Times to Key Contingency Areas

		Steaming days	
Place of departure (U.S.)	*Destination*	*20-knot speed*	*30-knot speed*
East Coast	North Atlantic	7	4⅔
East Coast	Mediterranean	10	6⅔
East Coast	Indian Ocean	24–18[a]	16–12[b]
West Coast	North Atlantic	31–18[c]	20⅔–12[d]
West Coast	Western Pacific	9	6
West Coast	Indian Ocean	24	16

Sources: Admiral James D. Watkins, U.S. Navy, *The Maritime Strategy* (Annapolis: U.S. Naval Institute, 1986), table 1, p. 10; and author's estimates.

a. The task force saves 6 days if it can use the Suez Canal.
b. The task force saves 4 days if it can use the Suez Canal.
c. The task force saves 13 days if it can use the Panama Canal.
d. The task force saves 8⅔ days if it can use the Panama Canal.

two ships in training or overhaul for every one on station, this would prevent the erosion in naval forces sought by its adversaries at home.

In an era when no real challenge to the Navy existed, such arguments may have been the only straws at which to grasp. However, there no longer is any serious case for claiming that nuclear weapons have made surface navies obsolete, or even that a large and powerful navy is unnecessary. A solid basis in force planning exists for the efficient force, or something like it, and if the best things in life were really free, the Navy's navy would be nice to have. Thus it no longer is necessary to play the permanent peacetime overseas presence game to protect the force structure. As far as navies fortify friends and deter potential enemies, they may actually be able to do so more effectively and at less cost by responding to crises and by appearing in distant waters at random intervals than by maintaining a steady, familiar presence that eventually becomes simply another part of the regular environment.

The Navy will object that under these conditions it cannot provide the rapid reaction to emergencies allegedly demanded by policymakers. But, as table 10-6 suggests, steaming times to major trouble spots are not that long, and the Navy has a noteworthy record of shortening them by its anticipation of orders and its early movement of ships to areas of concern. Furthermore, carriers need not be the only symbols of naval power. Some of the more modern amphibious ships are also impressively large and carry aircraft as well as Marines. Battleships create a striking impression, whatever else they may be good for. What are now called destroyers and frigates are large enough to attract attention. Even tall ships are deemed by some to create an impression. With a fleet the size of the efficient force, the U.S. Navy is unlikely to go unnoticed, however it may deploy and operate its ships. And there is a good chance that personnel problems will decline if the Navy is more selective in how it shows the flag.

Equal Performance, Lower Cost

In sum, a navy conservatively designed to pass realistic wartime tests will almost always prove sufficient to do well under the less demanding conditions of limited operations and peacetime presence. The U.S. Navy's fleet can certainly pass most of these tests, but the cost is high and Congress now may prove unwilling to pay it. The efficient force, by contrast, can pass the same tests and even obtain somewhat higher grades for nuclear deterrence and the support of overseas land-based forces. What is more, it can do all this for $120 billion less (in constant dollars) during the coming ten years.

Admittedly, the efficient force cannot perform all the missions demanded by the authors of *The Maritime Strategy*. But neither can the Navy's preferred fleet. Indeed, a gap exists between what U.S. naval authorities say they want to accomplish and the size of the fleet they have requested. There is also a gap between the cost of that fleet and the resources the Navy is likely to obtain in the years ahead. Both gaps need to be closed.

Benjamin Disraeli is supposed to have said, "When I want to read a novel I write one." The authors of *The Maritime Strategy* seem to have had much the same thought in mind. The time is past due, however, to put naval force planning on a basis of fact rather than fiction. A serious obligation still remains to demonstrate why the Navy cannot define more realistic missions and fulfill them with fewer than 600 ships.

Glossary of Ship Designators

AD	destroyer tender
AE/TAE	ammunition ship
AFS/TAFS	combat stores ship
AGS	sound testing barge
AO/TAO	oiler
AOE	multipurpose stores ship
AOR	replenishment oiler
AR	repair ship
ARS	salvage ship
AS	submarine tender
ASR	submarine rescue ship
ATF/TATF	fleet tug
ATS	salvage and rescue ship
BB	battleship
CG	guided-missile cruiser
CGN	nuclear powered guided-missile cruiser
CV	aircraft carrier
CVN	nuclear-powered aircraft carrier
DD	destroyer
DDG	guided-missile destroyer
FF	frigate
FFG	guided-missile frigate
LCAC	air-cushioned landing craft
LCC	amphibious command-control ship
LHA	amphibious assault ship (general purpose)
LHD	amphibious assault ship (multipurpose)
LKA	amphibious cargo assault ship
LPD	amphibious transport dock

LPH	amphibious assault ship (helicopter)
LSD	dock landing ship
LST	tank landing ship
MCM	mine countermeasures ship
MSH	mine hunter-sweeper ship
MSO	ocean minesweeper
PG/PHM	small patrol craft
SS	attack submarine
SSBN	nuclear-powered ballistic missile submarine
SSGN	nuclear powered cruise missile submarine
SSN	nuclear-powered attack submarine
TACS	crane ship
TAGM	range instrumentation ship
TAGOS	ocean surveillance ship (with sonar)
TAGS	fleet ballistic missile support ship
TAH	hospital ship
TAK	cargo ship
TAKS	maritime pre-positioning ship
TARC	cable ship
TAVB	aviation logistics support ship

Ship Designators by Major Function

	Nuclear retaliation
SSBN	nuclear-powered ballistic missile submarine
SSGN	nuclear-powered missile submarine
	General purpose combat
BB	battleship
CG	guided-missile cruiser
CGN	nuclear-powered guided-missile cruiser
CV	aircraft carrier
CVN	nuclear-powered aircraft carrier
DD	destroyer
DDG	guided-missile destroyer
FF	frigate
FFG	guided-missile frigate
PG/PHM	small patrol craft
SS	attack submarine
SSN	nuclear-powered attack submarine
	Amphibious warfare
LCAC	air-cushioned landing craft
LCC	command-control ship
LHA	general purpose assault ship
LHD	multipurpose assault ship
LKA	cargo assault ship
LPD	transport dock
LPH	helicopter assault ship
LSD	dock landing ship
LST	tank landing ship

	Mine warfare
MCM	mine countermeasures ship
MSH	mine hunter-sweeper ship
MSO	ocean minesweeper

	Underway replenishment
AE/TAE	ammunition ship
AFS/TAFS	combat stores ship
AO/TAO	oiler
AOE	multipurpose stores ship
AOR	replenishment oiler

	Material support
AD	destroyer tender
AR	repair ship
AS	submarine tender

	Fleet support
ARS	salvage ship
ASR	submarine rescue ship
ATF/TATF	fleet tug
ATS	salvage and rescue ship
TAGOS	ocean surveillance ship (with sonar)

	General support
AGS	sound testing barge
TACS	crane ship
TAGM	range instrumentation ship
TAGS	fleet ballistic missile support ship
TAH	hospital ship
TAK	cargo ship
TAKS	maritime pre-positioning ship
TARC	cable ship
TAVB	aviation logistics support ship

Other Department of the Navy Abbreviations

ARG	Marine amphibious group (ships)
AAW	anti-air warfare
ALCM	air-launched cruise missile
ALWT	advanced light-weight torpedo
ASCM	antiship cruise missile
ASROC	antisubmarine rocket
ASW	antisubmarine warfare
ASW/SOW	ASW stand-off weapon
C^3	command, control, and communications
C^3I	command, control, communications, and intelligence
CEP	circular error, probable
CIWS	close-in weapon system
CVBG	aircraft carrier battle group
CVV	medium-size aircraft carrier
ELF	extremely low frequency
FLTSATCOM	fleet satellite communications system
LAMPS	light airborne multipurpose system (helicopter)
LAV	light armored vehicle
LVT	amphibious assault vehicle
MAB	Marine amphibious brigade
MAF	Marine amphibious force
MAGTF	Marine air-ground task force
MAU	Marine amphibious unit
MPS	maritime pre-positioning ship
MSC	Military Sealift Command
PACOM	Pacific Command
SACEUR	supreme allied commander, Europe
SACLANT	supreme allied commander, Atlantic

SAM	surface-to-air missile
SLBM	submarine-launched ballistic missile
SLCM	sea-launched cruise missile
SLMM	submarine-launched mobile mine
SLOC	sea line of communications
SOSUS	sound surveillance underwater system
SUBACS	submarine advanced combat system
SURTASS	surveillance towed-array sonar system
TACTAS	tactical towed-array sonar
USCENTCOM	U.S. Central Command
USCINCCENT	commander in chief, U.S. Central Command
USCINCLANT	commander in chief, U.S. Atlantic Command
USCINCPAC	commander in chief, U.S. Pacific Command
VLA	vertical launch ASROC
VLS	vertical launch system

Table D-1. Soviet Attack Submarine Survivability as a Function of U.S. Antisubmarine Warfare Capabilities

U.S. ASW capabilities	Probability of submarines surviving and available to attack U.S. convoys			
	Month			
	1	*2*	*3*	*4*
None	1.0	1.0	1.0	1.0
Convoy escorts	.95	.86	.77	.7
Convoy escorts plus helicopters	.9	.735	.6	.49
Convoy escorts plus helicopters plus open-ocean search	.86	.63	.46	.34
Convoy escorts plus helicopters plus open-ocean search plus GIUK barrier[a]	.6	.22	.08	.03
Convoy escorts plus helicopters plus open-ocean search plus GIUK barrier[a] plus forward patrol	.54	.16	.05	.01

Source: Author's estimates.
a. Greenland, Iceland, and the United Kingdom.

Table E-1. Schedule for a Force of Twelve Deployable Aircraft Carriers[a]

1986		1987–90		1990–91		1991–2003[b]	
Hull number	Name	Hull number	Name	Hull number	Name	Hull number	Name
CV 41	Midway	...	...	...	...	...	...
CV43	Coral Sea[c]	...	...	...	...	...	...
CV59	Forrestal	CV59	Forrestal[c]	...	...	...	...
CV60	Saratoga	CV60	Saratoga	...	Saratoga[c]	...	...
CV61	Ranger	CV61	Ranger	CV60	Ranger	CV61	Ranger
CV62	Independence	CV62	Independence	CV61	Independence	CV62	Independence
CV63	Kitty Hawk	CV63	Kitty Hawk	CV62	Kitty Hawk	CV63	Kitty Hawk
CV64	Constellation	CV64	Constellation	CV63	Constellation	CV64	Constellation
CVN65	Enterprise	CVN65	Enterprise	CV64	Enterprise	CVN65	Enterprise
CV66	America	CV66	America	CVN65	America	CV66	America
CV67	Kennedy	CV67	Kennedy	CV66	Kennedy	CV67	Kennedy
CVN68	Nimitz	CVN68	Nimitz	CV67	Nimitz	CVN68	Nimitz
CVN69	Eisenhower	CVN69	Eisenhower	CVN68	Eisenhower	CVN69	Eisenhower
CVN70	Vinson	CVN70	Vinson	CVN69	Vinson	CVN70	Vinson
CVN71	Roosevelt	CVN71	Roosevelt	CVN70	Roosevelt	CVN71	Roosevelt
...	...	...	...	CVN71	Lincoln	CVN72	Lincoln
...	...	...	...	CVN72	...	CVN73	Washington

Sources: *Jane's Fighting Ships, 1985–86;* and author's estimates.

a. Starting in 1987 there would at all times be 12 deployable carriers and one in the service life extension program (SLEP).

b. CVN-74 and CVN-75, proposed in the FY1988 defense budget, are cancelled. No new carrier is funded until FY1995.

c. One of these three carriers would replace the Lexington as a fleet trainer; the other two would go into mothballs after 1991.

94   98